Contents

First published 2026
by Routledge
4 Park Square, Milton Park, Abingdon, Oxon OX14 4RN

and by Routledge
605 Third Avenue, New York, NY 10158

Routledge is an imprint of the Taylor & Francis Group, an informa business

British Library Cataloguing-in-Publication Data
A catalogue record for this book is available from the British Library

ISBN: 978-1-041-04233-4 (hbk)
ISBN: 978-1-041-04235-8 (pbk)
ISBN: 978-1-003-62744-9 (ebk)

DOI: 10.4324/9781003627449

Typeset in Times New Roman
by codeMantra

Goldsmith Banking: A History

Mabel Winter

Routledge
Taylor & Francis Group
LONDON AND NEW YORK

Goldsmith Banking: A History

In seventeenth-century England goldsmiths became what we would now recognise as bankers. Goldsmiths' shops sold not only gold and silver plate but also instruments of credit, such as bonds and bills of exchange, and offered 'safe' places to lodge capital at interest. As well as offering financial services to private individuals, goldsmith bankers also became trusted financial agents to the Crown.

Whilst some goldsmith banks still survive today, and the likes of Coutts are still associated with the Crown, the link between goldsmiths and banking is largely forgotten in modern Britain. This book explores the history of goldsmith banking from its early seventeenth-century origins, through its maturity in the Restoration, the collapse of significant goldsmith banks following the 1672 Stop on the Exchequer, and the continuation of goldsmith banking through the 'financial revolution', formation of the Bank of England, and beyond. It combines a general narrative with examples of specific goldsmith banks throughout the period to examine goldsmith bankers' practices, the instruments they dealt in and popularised, and the innovations in finance they instituted.

This concise introduction to goldsmith banking is ideal for students, academics, and those with a general interest in financial history or early modern London.

Mabel Winter received her PhD from the University of Sheffield and has since held positions at the University of Kent and the University of Sheffield. She is currently a postdoctoral research associate on the AHRC-funded project 'The Politics of the English Grain Trade, 1315-1815' at Oxford University. Mabel is the author of *Banking, Projecting and Politicking in Early Modern England.*

Routledge Focus on Financial History

About the Series

'Routledge Focus on Financial History' is a series of short form (20,000-50,000 words), accessible books telling the origin stories behind financial instruments, innovations and institutions. Each book provides historical context on the early development of topics such as investments, money, insurance, banking, central banks and financial theory. The emphasis is on engaging storytelling and clarity, making these topics interesting and understandable to a non-specialist audience.

The Tontine: A History
Andrew McDiarmid

Goldsmith Banking: A History
Mabel Winter

Acknowledgements

Writing this book has brought me back to the subject of my PhD and given me renewed enthusiasm for the history of early banking. I have found sources I didn't know existed and identified avenues of future research. I would like to thank the series editor Andrew McDiarmid for approaching me to contribute to the series and for his enthusiasm for the topic. I would also like to thank Andy Humphries and the editorial team at Routledge for their help throughout the publishing process.

I wish to express my gratitude to Professor Ling-Fan Li who very kindly allowed me to use the dataset she had gathered from the Goldsmiths' Assignment Books (E 406) at the National Archives, which features in Chapters 3 and 4. Gathering this data myself would have been extremely time consuming, and I would have been unable to carry out such detailed analysis without it. Another debt of gratitude is owed to Philip Winterbottom who first made me aware of Professor Li's dataset. Phil also very generously read and commented on most of the chapters, providing feedback and suggestions that have greatly improved the text.

I have used a variety of archives throughout the course of my research. I would like to thank all the archivists and staff who have responded to my queries and provided documents, particularly the National Archives in London, the Bodleian Archives in Oxford, Leicestershire Record Office, the NatWest Group Archives in Edinburgh, and the Barclays Group Archives in Manchester. This book has been written alongside my job as a postdoctoral researcher on an AHRC project, and thanks must go to Mike Bradick and the project for allowing me time to complete this work.

Thanks as ever to my wonderful family for their support, particularly my mum who is my greatest cheerleader. A mention must also go to my good friends Deborah and Phoebe, who thought this was a very different book! Final thanks go to Jamie, who, along with proofreading and commenting on the manuscript, has put up with years of me talking about early banking and has borne it all with patience and good humour! This book is for him.

1 The rise of goldsmith banking

Modern banking has its origins in medieval Italy, represented most famously in the family firms of Bardi, Peruzzi, and Medici. The German Fuggers were likewise important figures in the supply of banking services in the Middle Ages. In England foreign banks and financial institutions were commonly used in the medieval period to provide finance for monarchs. But it was not until the seventeenth century that English domestic banking was established. Whilst merchants, brokers, and scriveners were amongst the earliest progenitors of banking in England, it was the goldsmiths – members of the Goldsmiths' Company who were the authorised manufacturers, retailers, and regulators of plate and jewellery in England – who came to dominate the financial landscape by the mid-seventeenth century. Many of the practices they used and introduced underpin the modern banking system. Why and how goldsmiths rose to prominence as financiers, the practices they instituted, and their successes and failures are the subject of this book.

Existing studies of goldsmith banking are fragmented and widely dispersed. Goldsmith banking and goldsmith bankers often appear in broad narratives on finance in England, posited as the predecessors of the Bank of the England, as antecedents of the English 'financial revolution' at the turn of the eighteenth century, and as a part of the development of capitalism. Within these narratives goldsmiths are just a small part of the story, and the attention paid to goldsmith banking is minimal. Scholarship on goldsmith banking itself tends to focus on one specific goldsmith banker or a particular element or practice of goldsmith banking, and much of the work is in the form of stand-alone articles and book chapters. This book builds upon these existing studies and consolidates the history of goldsmith banking into one defining narrative, providing an overview of the origins, practices, challenges, and triumphs of goldsmith bankers.

The problem with studying any early bank is that source survival is limited. Very few ledgers, day books, notes, receipts, or correspondence survive for goldsmith banks before the 1690s, and even those after the 1690s are limited. Indeed, business records in general have a poor survival rate. Once a business closes, and particularly if it collapses or goes bankrupt, records tend

DOI: 10.4324/9781003627449-1

to be destroyed. To examine goldsmith banks and other early businesses, a variety of records must be studied. This includes the limited direct sources such as ledgers and accounts, as well as more indirect sources such as government records, court cases, and personal letters and diaries. Whilst the sources that survive provide a very small part of the picture, it is enough to reconstruct the story of goldsmith banking in England from the late sixteenth century into the eighteenth century.

The story of goldsmith banking is very much London-based. London in the early modern period, as is still the case today, was the financial heart of England. It was the centre of government and the royal court, the trading hub of the nation that drew in produce from a vast hinterland and attracted mercantile credit as well as the capital of the landed elite. Goldsmiths and goldsmith bankers were concentrated in specific areas of London, and their clientele were primarily from London and the surrounding areas. It was not until later in the eighteenth century that banking took off in England's provincial towns and cities.[1] Scotland, which exported some important Edinburgh goldsmith bankers to London at the turn of the eighteenth century, likewise lagged behind London in the development of banking before gaining ground in the eighteenth century.[2] Goldsmith banking is also a story that revolves around the wealthy elite. Early banking was the preserve of the 'monied' sort who had capital to deposit and invest, and who required financial services to assist with their business or estate.

The provision of financial services in England emerged organically and without state overview or design.[3] Prior to the formation of the Bank of England in 1694, early banking was private, not state sponsored or controlled. As will be shown, many of the financial practices carried out by goldsmiths were not even sanctioned by common law. In this regard, banking in England contrasted significantly with developments in Europe around a similar time, where exchange banks were established in Genoa in 1586, Venice in 1587, Milan in 1593, Amsterdam in 1609, and Hamburg in 1619.[4] Exchange banks were centralised institutions that administered state debt and were intended to regulate the money in circulation and facilitate commercial transactions amongst traders, not extend loans or expand the monetary supply as goldsmith banks did. As such the development of goldsmith banking, and subsequent financial institutions, has been described as 'peculiarly English'.[5]

What is meant by a 'banker'?

Before exploring the origins and rise of the goldsmith banker, the meaning of the term 'banker' in the seventeenth century must be clarified. The term banker was originally used to describe an exchange specialist or moneychanger, someone who made profits exchanging between foreign currencies. A good example is Sir Thomas Gresham, often described as 'banker' to Queen Elizabeth I, who exploited the discrepancies of foreign exchange to broker loans and reduce royal debt whilst enriching his own coffers. But Gresham facilitated loans only for the Crown and did not make loans or take deposits from other individuals.[6] Over the course of the seventeenth century in England, and as the activities of financiers such as goldsmiths and scriveners increased, the term banker took on a new definition: people who borrowed money from some people, in the form of deposits, and used that same money to lend to others at interest.[7] The use of banker and banking throughout this book follows this definition. The goldsmith bankers were not simple money lenders using their own funds to provide loans, nor were they brokers connecting those with money to lend with those requiring a loan and taking a fee for facilitating that connection. Instead, as will be explored in Chapter 2, goldsmiths were engaged primarily in drawing and discounting bills of exchange, dealing in government bonds, holding money on deposit, offering loans, and extending credit using paper notes.

When and how did goldsmiths become bankers?

It is impossible to pinpoint the first goldsmith who engaged in banking activities. However, historians generally agree that goldsmith bankers emerged at the turn of the seventeenth century. The transformation of goldsmiths into bankers can be split into two phases.

The first phase involved goldsmiths engaging in pawnbroking and the exchange of foreign and domestic coins. Early goldsmith banks have been described as 'elevated pawnshops', with customers using precious metals, plate, jewels, and stones as collateral for loans.[8] This activity could have started as early as the 1590s but, as will be shown in Chapter 2, was certainly well-established during the reign of James I.[9] In the early 1600s goldsmiths became associated with foreign exchange, changing foreign currencies, exploiting the discrepancies between coin, and engaging in the bullion trade. The profits from this activity would then be used to make loans and discount financial instruments.[10] By the 1620s there were growing distinctions between the 'naturall working Goldsmith' and the 'Exchanging Goldsmith'. This change caused grievances between members of the Goldsmiths' Company, leading to one petition to the governing body of the Company complaining about the 'new kind of trade' which had recently 'sprung up'.[11] Therefore, money lending and foreign exchange in the first phase were very much ancillary to the goldsmiths' primary trade in plate and jewellery, but the practices of goldsmiths were recognised to be changing.

The second phase occurred around the middle of the seventeenth century. It was around this time that goldsmiths' activities as bankers expanded, using funds deposited with them by some customers to make loans, in the form of paper instruments, to other customers. It was also during this period that bankers formed networks amongst themselves and began to accept each other's paper instruments through a process of inter-banker clearing, which allowed for greater circulation of paper notes in the London area.[12]

The catalyst to this second phase of expansion of goldsmiths' banking activities is routinely stated by historians to have been Charles I's 'seizure' of around £200,000 of coin and bullion in 1638, which had been deposited by London merchants for coining in the Mint. Following protests, Charles agreed to return the funds but made the return conditional upon a £40,000 loan from the merchants. Therefore, although he returned the money, Charles used it as leverage to enact a forced loan as part of his extra-parliamentary revenue-raising activities during the period of his Personal Rule. The actions of Charles I destroyed the reputation of the Mint as a safe depository, and indeed of any other government institution that could be accessed by the Crown.[13] Instead, merchants and other monied individuals turned to the goldsmiths as institutions that were out of reach of state interference – or at least outside the reach of direct state interference.[14] However, other historians, notably James Steven Rogers, have queried this course of events. Rogers labelled this series of events a 'myth' and argued that it was perfectly normal for the Crown to make temporary use of bullion at the Mint when it was short of money, and that Charles offered 'interest bearing exchequer receipts' for the bullion. According to Rogers, whilst 'the event made London merchants wary of financial dealings with the crown…it had nothing to do with money supposedly deposited at the Tower for safekeeping or with the development of the goldsmiths' business'.[15] Regardless of the catalytic force of this event, the Civil Wars that followed certainly enhanced the banking activities of the goldsmiths.

An influential pamphlet, *The Mystery of the New Fashioned Goldsmiths or Bankers* (1676), posited England's merchants and the events of the Civil Wars as key to the rise of goldsmith banking. Whilst the pamphlet castigated the goldsmith bankers, accusing them of 'Frauds, Oppressions, contempt of Government, and mischieves to the Publick', the story told of the rise of the goldsmith banker has become commonplace in accounts of English banking. The author stated that during the Civil Wars merchants lost their servants, with whom they usually entrusted their cash, to the army and were unwilling to use their apprentices as cashiers, so instead 'put their Cash into Goldsmiths hands to receive and pay for them'. The pamphlet also accused the goldsmiths of taking advantage of discrepancies in the weight of coins, using the instruments of their trade to clip metal from the coins to make a profit. With this profit the goldsmiths then began operating 'a running Cash', giving out loans and offering interest on money lodged with them. The author dubbed these individuals the 'new Goldsmiths', as opposed to working goldsmiths or even the exchanging goldsmiths, who had abandoned workmanship and the trade in plate and instead embraced the 'new Mystery' of banking. The activity of the new bankers extended to supplying the government with funds under Cromwell, and this activity increased following the Restoration.[16]

Whilst the pamphlet slightly sensationalises the rise of goldsmith banking – many of the practices it describes were well-established as early as the 1630s – the Civil Wars did accelerate the activities of goldsmith bankers and those depositing money with them. The reason behind this development has been put down to an increased need for security and safety amongst customers during the years of political disruption and warfare.[17] Goldsmiths' banking activities in the Civil War years were also likely encouraged by the decline in demand for plate and other gold and silver wares.[18] Lending money provided an alternate source of revenue, one that ultimately led to many goldsmith bankers distancing themselves from the physical work of their trade, although not without criticism. The exact trajectory cannot be mapped out but goldsmith banking was well-established by the mid-seventeenth century and Restoration of the monarchy in 1660.

Why goldsmiths?

Several aspects of the goldsmiths' trade lent themselves well to a transition into banking services. Goldsmiths were originally manufacturers of plate and jewellery, refiners of gold and silver, and had roles in government finance and the Mint. The Goldsmiths' Company first received a royal charter in the fourteenth century. Like other craft guilds, the Company regulated membership of the trade and enforced the rules and regulations governing the trade to ensure that members were carrying out fair practice and any wrongdoing was reported and punished. Membership was traditionally achieved via apprenticeship to a master goldsmith, which could be a period of up to seven years, in which time the apprentice was taught the skills and behaviours appropriate to that craft. Rules and regulations in the company concerned the right of search and assay over all wrought gold and silver, checking that the correct standard of metal alloy had been used. The Company's remit was not restricted to the capital. They also had the oversight of provincial goldsmiths who were required to take the company oath and were regularly overseen by wardens making tours of the provinces.[19] Goldsmiths therefore had established reputations for dealing in precious metals, which would naturally segue into dealing with coin and make their transition into banking appear quite natural.[20]

Another factor aiding goldsmiths' transition into banking was the networks formed through their trade which gave them access to potential customers. The goldsmiths served monied individuals, those who could afford plate and jewellery, who had surplus money to invest, and who might require financial services. Through dealings in plate and jewellery, goldsmiths were also familiar with large monetary transactions and chasing up debts. Indeed, their trade as bankers complemented their retail transactions, allowing customers with an account to pay more easily for goods via a transfer in the ledgers from credit to debit.[21]

Goldsmiths were also well-known individuals within the local London area. They built up good reputations through their trade, and individuals often held political offices and positions within the Goldsmiths' Company. Historians have shown that credit and reputation were key for both interpersonal and state finance in the seventeenth and eighteenth centuries.[22] Good credit relied on a reputation for honesty and fairness in economic and commercial dealings, and attributes such as having the freedom of the city through guild membership or holding a political office helped to further cultivate trust. Goldsmith banks were therefore not faceless corporations. The businesses were inseparable from the identity, character, and credit of their proprietors and, as will be seen in later chapters, many goldsmith bankers engaged in political and financial activities beyond the day-to-day job of banking.

The built environment and outward displays of financial standing were also important for the development of goldsmith banking. Goldsmiths had shops in prime locations that were accessible for the monied sort, and which had both practical and symbolic value. Goldsmiths' shops were located in the financial heart of the City of London, readily accessible to merchants and city tradesmen and near to the Royal Exchange, Goldsmiths' Hall, and, from 1694, the Bank of England. The shops were originally designed to store and market gold and silver wares and were fitted with safes, strong rooms, and secure display cabinets. Already deemed a safe place for the storage and display of gold and silver, it was not a giant leap to deem goldsmiths' shops as safe places for coin and money too. The counters and fittings came to facilitate the exchange of coin, paying in and collecting of money, and the trade in bills and bonds as well as selling and examining plate and jewellery. Aside from practicalities the shops were also important for the 'performance' of credit, acting as a physical representation of the proprietor's social status and credit.[23]

Other financial providers

Whilst the focus of this book is goldsmith bankers, they were not the only trade to engage in banking activities in England at this time and other providers deserve a mention. Scriveners, legal notaries who drew up legal and financial documents and so were exposed to knowledge of financial practices, were also regularly engaged in moneylending and brokerage activities. Indeed, one of the earliest London banks was the scrivener outfit of Robert Abbott, later taken over by his nephew Robert Clayton and his apprentice John Morris, which had its first premises in 1635 at the Flying Horse.[24] Like goldsmiths, scriveners operated within networks of wealthy individuals and had shops and offices where business could take place and be physically represented.[25] Scriveners were particularly well connected to landowners, who having used their conveyancing services began to also use the scrivener as a financial agent or banker. Scriveners similarly took deposits, made loans, and facilitated inland and overseas commercial transactions through bills of exchange. However, they were best known for developing the mortgage as a financial instrument, using their connections and expertise in land conveyancing to secure longer-term loans against property. In this regard most scriveners acted as brokers helping to match debtor and lender in person-to-person loans, managed the collection of rents for repayment, and managed estates, all for a fee.[26] Goldsmiths did deal in mortgages, but it was not common for them to do so until later in the seventeenth and eighteenth centuries.[27]

Scriveners are even less visible in the surviving records than goldsmith bankers. Aside from Frank Melton's forensic study of Clayton and Morris, money-scriveners have proven elusive. Melton argued that the scriveners 'lacked the continuity in their history that the goldsmiths had'. The medieval Scriveners' Company declined in the mid-sixteenth century as advances in printing signalled a decline in their scribal trade, but the scriveners' scribal services in legal transactions and conveyances led to the renewal of the guild in 1617. Most money-scriveners were 'small-scale financiers' and their records are either not extant or not easily identifiable.[28] Additionally, unlike the goldsmiths they were not involved in Crown finance and so there are no corresponding records found in government papers. As a result, it is the goldsmiths and not the scriveners who dominate the story of seventeenth-century finance.

Alongside goldsmiths and scriveners, merchants also acted as financiers in the sixteenth and seventeenth centuries. Merchants dealt with large amounts of money, had funds from which to supply loans, and were familiar with foreign exchange and the use of bills of exchange to facilitate foreign payments. Merchants loaned to the Crown as well as providing banking services to small groups of clients.[29] Whilst many merchants acted in the capacity of bankers, they were not known as bankers, and financial services were supplementary to their primary trade.[30]

The need for more or greater financial institutions in the seventeenth century was further highlighted by numerous proposals for other financial institutions, both private and state-sponsored, in the second half of the seventeenth century. Four different types of proposal circulated: the Lumbard bank, similar to a pawnshop where credit was offered on the basis of a variety of goods taken in; land banks, based on the security of land recorded in a registry; banks using government revenues, the Bank of England being a notable success of this category; and banks based on commercial obligations, which often entailed the establishment of a network of banks across the country to facilitate trade transactions. Most proposals were not put into practice, but their existence demonstrates the widespread recognition of the need for financial innovation to meet nascent and growing demand.[31]

Why did this happen in the seventeenth century?

The goldsmith bankers emerged in a period of great economic growth and of economic turmoil. From the mid-to-late sixteenth century onwards there was increased economic activity in England, partly due to global exploration and colonial ventures. Real wages rose as 'a consequence of improvements and innovations in agricultural, extractive, processing and manufacturing industry and in commercial and financial practice'.[32] At the same time, warfare between financially and politically expanding states placed greater fiscal burdens upon monarchs and governments to raise revenue and improve their financial situation. In England there was a shortage of coin, partly due to the debasements enacted throughout the Tudor period. The Crown, in need of money for warfare, increased the quantity of coin whilst decreasing its quality by stripping out an amount of metal from each coin to produce more, leading to inflation. Subsequent recoinage failed to tackle ongoing, and unrelated, inflation, and the monetary system itself lacked the sophistication required to facilitate the growing trade networks and increasingly commercial nature of the country.[33] Goldsmiths' wealth and knowledge of precious metals and foreign exchange meant they were well placed to offer solutions to these challenges.

A development key to the rise of goldsmith banking, and of banking and finance in general, was changes made to, and compliance with, English usury laws. Usury, or making a profit from moneylending by charging interest, had long been practiced but was widely condemned and illegal. A Henrician statute of 1545 had allowed usury up to 10%, but this was swiftly repealed by an Edwardian statute of 1552, which once again outlawed all usury. Attitudes towards usury began to change around the mid-sixteenth century as the economic landscape in England expanded. The primary opposition to usury originally came from theologians, who saw God's law and secular law as inseparable. Profit made from lending money was viewed as exploiting the borrower and sinful on the part of the lender, particularly for loans to the lower sort of people, which should be done out of charity and not for profit. Some exceptions were allowed. If a borrower was late repaying their loan, then the lender could claim interest, but this interest only became due after the repayment date had passed and had not been contracted for originally. Also, if the lender was engaging in risk with the borrower, for example if the loan was for a trading venture that may or may not produce a profit, then they could charge interest. There were also many ways in which lenders circumvented the usury laws, disguising interest under a variety of practices and exploiting legal loopholes.[34]

As the sixteenth century progressed the debate surrounding usury morphed from theological debates into economic and legal debates, with thinkers recognising the widespread use of loans at interest and the economic benefits it brought. In 1571 an Elizabethan statute technically upheld the illegality of usury, but loans made at 10% interest or below essentially went unpunished. This meant that the main outcome of the act was to reduce interest rates, which had previously been much higher, rather than outlaw usury entirely. Charging interest was by the early seventeenth century a normal part of economic activities, and subsequent laws only ever reduced the legal limit of interest rather than revoking the practice of charging interest itself. The legal limit was reduced to 8% in 1624, 6% in 1651, and 5% from 1714.[35] The legal limit did not apply to loans made to the Crown, as monarchs could not be sued in their own courts. The Crown relied on loans in the seventeenth century to combat its low revenue-raising capabilities. However, loans to the Crown were far riskier than an average commercial loan and so greater incentives were required to attract capital, such as a higher rate of interest.[36] As will be shown, the goldsmiths' business model, at least until 1672, relied on the higher interest charged on Crown loans.

The rest of this book

The seventeenth century was a key period for the financial history of England, and the goldsmiths were at the heart of many of these developments, laying the foundations for modern banking in Britain as we know it. The following chapter examines the financial practices of goldsmith bankers, looking at the financial instruments they used, their use of the fractional reserve system to extend credit, and how they formed a network of bankers to facilitate the circulation of notes. Chapter 3 explores the earliest goldsmith bankers and innovators in the trade, including evidence of their size and clientele. Chapter 4 deals with the causes and effects of the 1672 'Stop on the Exchequer', when the Crown suspended payments on certain modes of debt, and its impact on goldsmith banking. Chapter 5 examines the later goldsmith bankers who either survived or were exempt from the effects of 1672, the different practices they employed and evidence of their size and clientele. Finally, the last chapter explores the legacy of goldsmith banking and its place within the wider history of finance in England.

Notes

1 L.S. Pressnell, *Country Banking in the Industrial Revolution* (Oxford: Clarendon Press, 1956).
2 J.G. Checkland, *Scottish Banking: A History, 1695–1973* (Glasgow: Collins, 1975), Chapters 1 and 2; Andrew McDiarmid, *Credit, Currency, and Capital: The Scottish Financial Revolution, 1690–1727* (London: Routledge, 2023).
3 Christine Desan, *Making Money: Coin, Currency, and the Coming of Capitalism* (Oxford: Oxford University Press, 2014), p. 12; Stephen Quinn, 'Goldsmith-Banking: Mutual Acceptance and Interbank Clearing in Restoration London', *Explorations in Economic History* 34 (1997), pp. 411–32.
4 Henry Roseveare, *The Financial Revolution 1660–1760* (London: Longman, 1991), p. 10; Stephen Quinn, *How a Ledger became a Central Bank: A Monetary History of the Bank of Amsterdam* (Cambridge: Cambridge University Press, 2024).
5 Eric Kerridge, *Trade and Banking in Early Modern England* (Manchester: Manchester University Press, 1988), pp. 2, 68.
6 John Guy, *Gresham's Law: The Life and World of Queen Elizabeth I's Banker* (London: Profile Books, 2019); Raymond de Roover, *Gresham on Foreign Exchange: An Essay on Early English Mercantilism with the Text of Sir Thomas Gresham's Memorandum for the Understanding of the Exchange* (Oxford: Oxford University Press, 1949).

7 Frank T. Melton, *Sir Robert Clayton and the Origins of English Deposit Banking 1658–1685* (Cambridge: Cambridge University Press, 1986), pp. 8–11.
8 Peter Temin and Hans-Joachim Voth, *Prometheus Shackled: Goldsmith Banks and England's Financial Revolution after 1700* (Oxford: Oxford University Press, 2013), p. 72.
9 Kerridge, *Trade and Banking*, p. 66.
10 Jongchul Kim, 'How Modern Banking Originated: The London Goldsmith-Bankers' Institutionalisation of Trust', *Business History* 53 (2011), p. 942.
11 State Papers Online, SP 16/107 f.33, Lists of [London] Goldsmiths, distinguishing those which make jewels and rings from those which make "plate and vessel;" with various questions to be addressed to them, 13 June 1628; SP 14/163 f.14, Commonalty of Goldsmiths. Petition of the Commonalty of Goldsmiths to the Warden and Assistants of the Goldsmiths' Company, April 1624.
12 Quinn, 'Goldsmith-Banking'; For more, see Chapter 2.
13 Roseveare, *Financial Revolution*, p. 11; R.D. Richards, *The Early History of Banking in England* (London: Routledge, 2012 reprint), pp. 35–6; Glyn Davies, *A History of Money* (Cardiff: University of Wales Press, 2016), pp. 286–289; J. Keith Horsefield, *British Monetary Experiments 1650–1710* (London: G. Bell and Sons, 1960), p. 99; Moshe Milevsky, *The Day the King Defaulted: Financial Lessons from the Stop of the Exchequer in 1672* (Cham: Palgrave, 2017), pp. 52–3.
14 The impact of indirect interference is discussed in Chapter 4.
15 James Steven Rogers, *The Early History of the Law of Bills and Notes: A Study of the Origins of Anglo-American Commercial Law* (Cambridge: Cambridge University Press, 1995), p. 118.
16 *The Mystery of the New Fashioned Goldsmiths or Bankers. Their Rise, Growth, State, and Decay* (1676).
17 Richards, *Early History*, p. 36; Roseveare, *The Financial Revolution*, p. 12; Ben Coates, *The Impact of the English Civil War on the Economy of London, 1642–50* (London: Routledge, 2016), pp. 84–5; Davies, *History of Money*, p. 250; Kerrridge, *Trade and Banking*, p. 69; Desan, *Making Money*, p. 244.
18 David Mitchell, 'Innovation and the Transfer of Skill in the Goldsmiths' Trade in Restoration London', in David Mitchell (ed.), *Goldsmiths, Silversmiths and Bankers: Innovation and the Transfer of Skill, 1550 to 1750* (London: Alan Sutton Publishing, 1995), p. 11; Coates, *Impact of the English Civil War*, pp. 207–8.
19 Mitchell, 'Innovation', p. 20; Kerridge, *Trade and Banking*, pp. 69–70; David Mitchell, *The Wider Goldsmiths' Trade in Elizabethan and Stuart London* (London: Ad Ilissum, 2024), Chapter 2.
20 Rogers, *Early History*, p. 119.
21 Mitchell, 'Innovation', p. 15.
22 For example, Craig Muldrew, *The Economy of Obligation: The Culture of Credit and Social Relations in Early Modern England* (Basingstoke: Macmillan, 1988); Anne L. Murphy, 'Performing Public Credit at the Eighteenth-Century Bank of England', *Journal of British Studies* 58 (2019), pp. 58–78; Margot C. Finn, *The Character of Credit: Personal Debt in English Culture, 1740–1914* (Cambridge: Cambridge University Press, 2003).
23 Murphy, 'Performing Public Credit', pp. 58–78; Claire Walsh, 'The Design of London Goldsmiths' Shops in the Early Eighteenth Century', in David Mitchell (ed.), *Goldsmiths, Silversmiths and Bankers: Innovation and the Transfer of Skill, 1550 to 1750* (London: Alan Sutton Publishing, 1995), pp. 96–111; Perry Gauci, *The London Private Banker: A Social History* (Oxford: Oxford University Press, 2025), pp. 56–70.
24 Richards, *Early History*, pp. 15–17; Coates, *Impact of the English Civil War*, pp. 85–6; Melton, *Sir Robert Clayton*.

25 Roseveare, *Financial Revolution*, p. 21; Youssef Cassis and Phillip L. Cottrell, *Private Banking in Europe: Rise, Retreat, and Resurgence* (Oxford: Oxford University Press, 2015), pp. 31–2.
26 Melton, *Sir Robert Clayton*, pp. 21, 53–6, 126–57; Kim, 'How Modern Banking Originated', p. 946.
27 Cassis and Cottrell, *Private Banking in Europe*, p. 37.
28 Melton, *Sir Robert Clayton*, pp. 23–8.
29 Richards, *Early History*, pp. 8–11; Kerridge, *Trade and Banking*, pp. 46–7.
30 One exception being Thompson and Company: See Mabel Winter, *Banking, Projecting, and Politicking in Early Modern England* (Cham: Palgrave Macmillan, 2022).
31 Horsefield, *British Monetary Experiments*, pp. xvii–xviii, 93–217.
32 Kerridge, *Trade and Banking*, p. 86.
33 Desan, *Making Money*, pp. 114, 232–4, 237; Kerridge, *Trade and Banking*, p. 85.
34 Norman Jones, *God and the Moneylenders: Usury Law in Early Modern England* (Oxford: Basil Blackwell, 1989). Also see Raymond de Roover, 'What Is Dry Exchange? A Contribution to the Study of English Mercantilism', *Journal of Political Economy* 52 (1944), pp. 250–66.
35 Jones, *God and the Moneylenders*, Chapter 4; Richards, *Early History*, pp. 19–21, 213–5; Temin and Voth, *Prometheus Shackled*, p. 44.
36 Milevsky, *Day the King Defaulted*, p. 68; Stephen Quinn, 'Tallies or Reserves? Sir Francis Child's Balance between Capital Reserves and Extending Credit to the Crown, 1685–1695', *Business and Economic History* 23 (1994), p. 41; Bruce G. Carruthers, *City of Capital: Politics and Markets in the English Financial Revolution* (Princeton: Princeton University Press, 1996), p. 55; Jones, *God and the Moneylenders*, pp. 51–2.

Bibliography

Primary sources

State Papers Online, SP 16/107 f.33, Lists of [London] Goldsmiths, distinguishing those which make jewels and rings from those which make "plate and vessel;" with various questions to be addressed to them, 13 June 1628.

The Mystery of the New Fashioned Goldsmiths or Bankers. Their Rise, Growth, State, and Decay (1676).

Books, edited collections, and journal articles

Carruthers, Bruce G., *City of Capital: Politics and Markets in the English Financial Revolution* (Princeton: Princeton University Press, 1996).

Cassis, Youssef and Phillip L. Cottrell, *Private Banking in Europe: Rise, Retreat, and Resurgence* (Oxford: Oxford University Press, 2015).

Checkland, J.G., *Scottish Banking: A History, 1695–1973* (Glasgow: Collins, 1975).

Coates, Ben, *The Impact of the English Civil War on the Economy of London, 1642–50* (London: Routledge, 2016).

Davies, Glyn, *A History of Money* (Cardiff: University of Wales Press, 2016)

Desan, Christine, *Making Money: Coin, Currency, and the Coming of Capitalism* (Oxford: Oxford University Press, 2014).

de Roover, Raymond, 'What Is Dry Exchange? A Contribution to the Study of English Mercantilism', *Journal of Political Economy* 52 (1944), pp. 250–66.

de Roover, Raymond, *Gresham on Foreign Exchange: An Essay on Early English Mercantilism with the Text of Sir Thomas Gresham's Memorandum for the Understanding of the Exchange* (Oxford: Oxford University Press, 1949).

Finn, Margot C., *The Character of Credit: Personal Debt in English Culture, 1740–1914* (Cambridge: Cambridge University Press, 2003).

Gauci, Perry, *The London Private Banker: A Social History* (Oxford: Oxford University Press, 2025).

Guy, John, *Gresham's Law: The Life and World of Queen Elizabeth I's Banker* (London: Profile Books, 2019).

Horsefield, J. Keith, *British Monetary Experiments 1650–1710* (London: G. Bell and Sons, 1960).

Jones, Norman, *God and the Moneylenders: Usury Law in Early Modern England* (Oxford: Basil Blackwell, 1989).

Kerridge, Eric, *Trade and Banking in Early Modern England* (Manchester: Manchester University Press, 1988).

Kim, Jongchul, 'How Modern Banking Originated: The London Goldsmith-Bankers' Institutionalisation of Trust', *Business History* 53 (2011), pp. 939–59.

McDiarmid, Andrew, *Credit, Currency, and Capital: The Scottish Financial Revolution, 1690–1727* (London: Routledge, 2023).

Melton, Frank T., *Sir Robert Clayton and the Origins of English Deposit Banking 1658–1685* (Cambridge: Cambridge University Press, 1986).

Milevsky, Moshe, *The Day the King Defaulted: Financial Lessons from the Stop of the Exchequer in 1672* (Cham: Palgrave, 2017).

Mitchell, David, 'Innovation and the Transfer of Skill in the Goldsmiths' Trade in Restoration London', in David Mitchell (ed.), *Goldsmiths, Silversmiths and Bankers: Innovation and the Transfer of Skill, 1550 to 1750* (London: Alan Sutton Publishing, 1995), pp. 5–22.

Mitchell, David, *The Wider Goldsmiths' Trade in Elizabethan and Stuart London* (London: Ad Ilissum, 2024).

Muldrew, Craig, *The Economy of Obligation: The Culture of Credit and Social Relations in Early Modern England* (Basingstoke: Macmillan, 1988).

Murphy, Anne L., 'Performing Public Credit at the Eighteenth-Century Bank of England', *Journal of British Studies* 58 (2019), pp. 58–78.

Pressnell, L.S., *Country Banking in the Industrial Revolution* (Oxford: Clarendon Press, 1956).

Quinn, Stephen, 'Tallies or Reserves? Sir Francis Child's Balance between Capital Reserves and Extending Credit to the Crown, 1685–1695', *Business and Economic History* 23 (1994), pp. 39–51.

Quinn, Stephen, 'Balances and Goldsmith-Bankers: The Co-ordination and Control of Inter-banker Debt Clearing in Seventeenth-century London', in David Mitchell (ed.), *Goldsmiths, Silversmiths and Bankers: Innovation and the Transfer of Skill, 1550 to 1750* (London: Alan Sutton Publishing, 1995), pp. 53–76.

Quinn, Stephen, 'Goldsmith-Banking: Mutual Acceptance and Interbank Clearing in Restoration London', *Explorations in Economic History* 34 (1997), pp. 411–32.

Quinn, Stephen, *How a Ledger became a Central Bank: A Monetary History of the Bank of Amsterdam* (Cambridge: Cambridge University Press, 2024).

Richards, R.D., *The Early History of Banking in England* (London: Routledge, 2012 reprint).

Rogers, James Steven, *The Early History of the Law of Bills and Notes: A Study of the Origins of Anglo-American Commercial Law* (Cambridge: Cambridge University Press, 1995).

Roseveare, Henry, *The Financial Revolution 1660–1760* (London: Longman, 1991).

Temin, Peter and Hans-Joachim Voth, *Prometheus Shackled: Goldsmith Banks and England's Financial Revolution after 1700* (Oxford: Oxford University Press, 2013).

Walsh, Claire, 'The Design of London Goldsmiths' Shops in the Early Eighteenth Century', in David Mitchell (ed.), *Goldsmiths, Silversmiths and Bankers: Innovation and the Transfer of Skill, 1550 to 1750* (London: Alan Sutton Publishing, 1995), pp. 96–111.

Winter, Mabel, *Banking, Projecting, and Politicking in Early Modern England: The Rise and Fall of Thompson and Company 1671–1678* (Cham: Palgrave Macmillan, 2022).

2 The practices of goldsmith bankers

In modern Britain, paper money is now old hat. Due to recent advances in technology, electronic means of payment, including contactless payments, have largely superseded the use of paper money. Cheques are even more antiquated, as are travellers' cheques for spending abroad. But in early seventeenth-century England, money was coin made of precious metals, and there was a finite amount of it. Many financial transactions were therefore carried out through interpersonal credit networks, which represented the theoretical transfer of coin but only used physical coin to settle final debts,[1] and paper instruments. Paper financial instruments were largely the preserve of merchants trading abroad. However, over the course of the seventeenth century paper financial instruments were increasingly used in everyday commercial transactions. Fully functioning paper money would not be in existence for years to come, and fiat money – money completely unlinked from precious metals – centuries in the future. But paper instruments altered the way in which finance and banking operated in England, and goldsmiths played an important part in that story.

The financial activities of goldsmiths, historians have suggested, originated in pawnbroking, making loans on the security of plate or jewellery.[2] This practice only gradually faded out, and pawnbroking remained a key element of goldsmith banking into the early eighteenth century.[3] In pawnbroking, a loan would be advanced against the value of plate, with the plate acting as a security for the creditor should the debtor default on repayment.[4] Goldsmiths also engaged in foreign exchange and the trade in bullion, exploiting discrepancies between the metallic content of domestic and foreign coin and between exchange rates. Domestic coin could also be exploited due to the numerous debasements of the coinage over the Tudor period, which meant that purer coins, with a greater metallic content, could be clipped (the edges shaved off) to melt down for bullion.[5] Goldsmiths, who were trained to assess the quality and quantity of precious metal, were well placed to engage in the bullion trade and were active for many decades prior to and after their expansion into banking.[6]

DOI: 10.4324/9781003627449-2

Whilst pawnbroking, foreign exchange, and the bullion trade were important aspects of goldsmith banking, this chapter focusses on paper financial instruments that became increasingly dominant across the seventeenth century, and which were central to the operation of goldsmith banking and the progress of English banking more widely. Goldsmith bankers dealt in paper bonds and bills of exchange, discounted government tallies, accepted cheques, and circulated their own form of paper notes. To extend credit, goldsmiths instituted the practice of fractional reserve, and to increase the circulation of credit they formed a network whereby they accepted each other's notes. This activity was underpinned by ever more detailed and sophisticated account keeping, which was often organised on the principles of double-entry bookkeeping and was vital for bankers to make decisions about credit and lending and keep track of repayments and defaults.[7] This chapter explores goldsmiths' financial practices and the innovative processes they instituted.

Government tallies

Tallies were sticks made of hazel wood that originally recorded receipt of payment into the Exchequer by a revenue collector but in the seventeenth century were increasingly used by the Exchequer to make payments. A tally would be issued to a creditor who had provided goods or services to the Crown, who would then present the tally to the named revenue collector at a specified date, once the revenue had been collected, and receive payment.[8] Tallies were also issued to provide funds for departmental treasurers, who would use them to pay creditors and suppliers. The wider use of the tally as a form of credit depended on the secondary market. Holders of tallies could assign them to pay their creditors and suppliers, or they could discount them at the shops of goldsmith bankers. Goldsmiths offered a discounted amount of ready cash for the tally below its face value and then held it until maturity to collect the full value. Essentially the goldsmith banker was making a loan to the holder of the tally, providing funds on the security of it and gaining significant interest from the discrepancy between the discounted value and the full value. Tallies operated in this way with 'no statutory guarantee of transferability' or 'legal security', so they were endorsed and transferred freely but without any legal backing.[9] The process of discounting was vital in providing greater liquidity – the ability to interchange financial instruments with other assets or money – to instruments of government debt.

Instruments of government debt had to follow strict and complicated procedures, which tied up the money loaned for a significant amount of time. They were therefore unattractive to the public. Goldsmith bankers acted as intermediaries, taking in deposits from the public and pooling those funds to then make larger loans to the government via tallies. Customer deposits would receive the statutory rate of interest (6%), whilst loans to the government and Crown would come at much higher rates of interest (up to and over 10%). The goldsmiths dealt with the Exchequer and provided the depositor with a more liquid form of investment, whilst profiting from the discrepancy between the interest rate offered on deposits and received on loans.[10] Not all goldsmith bankers loaned to the Crown or dealt in tallies, but the interest-bearing deposit accounts offered by bankers involved in government debt undoubtedly acted as a magnet to attract customers to part with their cash. Those not dealing in government debt did not offer interest-bearing deposit accounts to customers.[11]

Government tallies were particularly important for military funding, which required large sums of money at particular times that could not be met by the slow trickle of taxes across the year. C. D. Chandaman gives the example of a tally issued to the Navy Treasurer in 1664, which was only cashed by the corresponding customs famers over three years later, during which time it had probably been passed from hand-to-hand as payment, used as security against a loan, and discounted with a goldsmith banker.[12] Indeed, departmental Treasurers, such as Samuel Pepys, frequented goldsmith banks 'to borrow a little money upon a tally'.[13] In providing tallies and paper instruments to departments and suppliers, Aaron Graham argued that the government shifted the burden of raising short-term credit onto others. It was the suppliers and receivers of government tallies and paper who then had to find a way to convert them into cash, relying on speculators, financiers, and bankers to accept the tallies or paper instruments as security for loans. Using evidence from eighteenth-century equity courts, Graham revealed the long lines of credit this could inspire, as debts were collateralised, packaged up, and used to secure different loans which matured at different times to spread that money further. In short, when money from one loan came in, it would filter through a credit network, satisfying various obligations on the way.[14]

Bills obligatory, bonds, and bills of exchange

The most common financial instruments for money lending and trade were the bill obligatory, bond, and bill of exchange. A bill obligatory was an agreement whereby the recipient of money promised to repay the debt at a later, specified, date. The bill recorded the names of creditor and debtor, the amount of money involved, the date for repayment, and the date it was created. For further security a bond could be attached in which a penalty for non-payment was added to the bill obligatory. If the debtor did not repay the full amount on the specified date, then the creditor could demand a penalty fee, which could be in excess of double the amount of the original debt. Typically, these documents were drawn up by scriveners. They represented a legally binding contract and were witnessed and sealed.[15]

One of the most useful and well-known financial instruments for trade was the bill of exchange, which enabled the exchange of money over both short and long distances without the physical risk of transporting specie. The bill of exchange was less formal than the bill obligatory and did not require a seal or witnesses. Bills of exchange originated in the trade fairs of medieval Europe and were used extensively by merchants in commercial transactions. Bills of exchange were reciprocal and contractual – they required a trading relationship to function – and they involved an exchange rate of a certain amount of home currency for a certain amount of foreign currency.[16] London goldsmiths used their knowledge of exchange rates and foreign coin, and their links to factors or agents abroad, to make or receive international payments by means of bills of exchange on behalf of their clients.[17]

The bill of exchange could be used to pay a specific person only, or it could include a clause stating it was payable to the named person or their order. Including the clause 'or order' meant that should the holder of a bill need or want to pay someone else before their money became due for repayment, they could assign the bill to a third party (their order, the assignee) by writing that person's name on the back of the bill. When the bill became due it was the assignee who collected payment. It was common for bills to be assigned multiple times, with the name of each assignee being ascribed to the back of the bill.[18] Like government tallies, bills of exchange were payable at a specified future date and could also be discounted. If the holder needed money before the bill became due, they could assign it to a goldsmith banker (their order), accepting a lesser amount upfront than the face value of the bill. When the bill became due, the goldsmith banker presented it for repayment, receiving the full amount and therefore making a profit.[19]

Bills of exchange were originally reserved for foreign payments, but across the seventeenth century they were commonly drawn and payable within Britain, known as inland bills of exchange. These bills followed the same principles as foreign bills but over shorter distances and without an exchange of currencies.[20] Local suppliers might prefer to be paid via an inland bill payable in London if they had need of funds there.[21] Like foreign or 'outland' bills of exchange, goldsmiths discounted inland bills, providing funds in advance of the bill becoming due and profiting from the difference in price.

Legality

The problem with bills and bonds was that whilst they had been commonly used as forms of payment and assigned from person to person for decades, the common law did not recognise their assignability until the 1650s nor their negotiability until the early 1700s. It took time for the law to catch up with, and codify, common practice. Assignability and negotiability were desirable features of paper instruments because they increased liquidity. Instead of immediately being presented for repayment, the debt could circulate and facilitate more transactions.

To be assignable meant that the bill could be legally transferred to another person – using the named recipient 'or order' clause – who would then have the same rights to the money as the assignor. Bills of exchange were in use in England from at least the early sixteenth century and were frequently assigned. However, bills could only legally be assigned once. The named recipient could assign the bill to their order, but their order could not further reassign the bill. The original contract named the creditor, debtor, and one assignee, so later assignees were not recognised as having a legal claim to the bill. However, merchants, who had been assigning and reassigning bills as part of their normal trading practices for decades, believed the final assignee had as much right to the money as the original named recipient. It was argued that this mercantile custom, commonly referred to as the 'law merchant', should be recognised at common law as it represented common practice not just for merchants but for all who used paper bills. From the mid-seventeenth century, English common law gradually adopted this position.[22] Each assignee became legally entitled to the money and could reassign the bill to others. As the bill was assigned, each assignee named on the bill became liable for its payment should the acceptor or drawer default.[23]

Whilst assignability of bills was legally recognised in the seventeenth century, negotiability was not legally recognised until 1704. Negotiability did away with the need for assigning a document, it simply passed from hand-to-hand under the clause payable to named recipient 'or bearer'. The payment was due to whoever physically held the bill. The payable to named recipient or bearer clause was not commonly used amongst merchants nor recognised as part of mercantile custom.[24] In common law, without written assignment there was no proof that the rights to the money had been transferred by the original named recipient. Whilst legal developments are important, lack of legal transferability did not stop the use of assignable and negotiable instruments in practice. Individuals put their trust in the system and those they were dealing with that written obligations would be honoured. One of the main documents to use the bearer clause was the promissory note, which was used extensively by goldsmiths in the seventeenth century.

Goldsmiths' notes

Goldsmiths did not invent promissory notes, but they did use them extensively and popularise their use in banking.[25] Promissory notes were even more casual and informal than bills, comprising a promise to pay rather than an instruction to a third party to pay, and had been used in trade for years prior to the goldsmiths' use of them. There was no need to assign notes by writing names on the back, as all notes were issued to the named recipient 'or bearer', so whoever physically held the note had a claim to the money it represented. Lack of a named recipient depersonalised credit instruments. The debt was cleared as the note passed from hand-to-hand, rather than making each person it passed to liable for payment as was the case with the 'or order' clause. This meant the debt could change hands without the knowledge of the creditor.[26]

Promissory notes issued by goldsmiths, often referred to as goldsmiths' notes, began as receipts for funds deposited in the bank. Upon receiving a customer's deposit, the goldsmith banker would issue a note stating that they promised to pay that customer the amount deposited. The deposits were either demand deposits that could be recalled at any time, or time deposits that could be withdrawn after a specified notice period. Over time the receipts evolved into transferrable paper instruments, representing money held on account at a goldsmith's shop and used to make payments.[27] As well as acknowledgements and instruments of receipt, promissory notes were issued when providing loans or discounting bills of exchange or government tallies instead of cash. The earliest extant goldsmiths' note, combining a receipt with a promise to repay, is from 1654 and was issued by Cromwellian goldsmith Field Whorwood.[28]

Unlike bills of exchange, which could circulate internationally, during the seventeenth century goldsmiths' notes circulated locally in London. Their circulation depended on those accepting the notes trusting the banker who had originally issued it. The local nature of notes was the reason they often used the bearer clause – those accepting the notes were aware of the reputation of the banker who had issued it and were willing to accept it based on trust. The same cannot be said for bills of exchange that circulated nationally or internationally, where greater distance between creditor and debtor decreased trust and increased risk, and the names of assignees on the back of notes (to order) offered an extra layer of security.[29]

As mentioned above in relation to bills of exchange, negotiability of notes, including the named recipient or bearer clause, was not fully accepted by law until 1704. The statute decreed that to 'encourage trade and commerce', promissory notes, including goldsmiths' notes, would be given the same protection in law as other forms of bills.[30] Despite their lack of legality, drawn notes and goldsmiths' notes had been used for decades prior to this.

Running cashes

To facilitate payments by bills and notes, goldsmith bankers in London held customers' money on account. A country gentleman or provincial landowner, for example, could then direct people to their bank for payment, or could withdraw money in person from their account when they were in London for the season.[31] Goldsmiths conducting these practices were said to hold 'running cashes', similar to a modern current account credit balance, from which their customers could draw, requesting the goldsmith to pay named individuals via written instructions. Goldsmiths holding running cashes were common from the mid-seventeenth century, but, as will be shown in Chapter 3, the practice of goldsmiths acting as an agent for country gentry was evident at the end of the sixteenth century. Notes used to direct payments in the earlier period, usually called drawn notes, have been described as forerunners of the cheque, but could also be likened to inland bills of exchange.[32] Running cashes could also be used to pay for the goldsmiths' retail wares – plate and jewellery – 'transferring' the money directly in the books to pay for purchases. The use of notes and running cashes expanded credit networks, allowing one deposit of coin to be used in multiple transactions, and underpinned the fractional reserve system utilised by goldsmith bankers.

Fractional reserve

Fractional reserve banking is the system which underpins modern banking around the world, but it was not common in London until the mid-to-late seventeenth century. In a fractional reserve system, a bank accepts deposits from individuals creating accounts from which they can withdraw or pay out money up to the value deposited and often beyond in the form of an overdraft. The deposited money of individuals is then pooled by the bank to form a fund which it can invest in other schemes and from which it can offer loans to other individuals. The money appears in the account books twice, both as an amount deposited by a customer in coin and an amount loaned out to another customer in paper notes – what Jongchul Kim calls 'a double-ownership scheme', whereby two individuals simultaneously own the same thing. The fractional reserve system created legal disputes over ownership and fraud. However, in England, common law supported the idea that deposits were loans to the bank, and that the bankers were free to use that money in their own names to create profit from investment and lending. The bank retains, or *reserves*, only a fraction of the deposited money as security to facilitate an estimated maximum level of cash withdrawals of its depositors. In so doing, a fractional reserve bank increases the amount of money in circulation.[33]

The success of fractional reserve banking relies on the premise that not all depositors will request their deposited funds back at one and the same time. The bank would retain enough reserve funds to meet requests from some, but not all, depositors. Under normal circumstances this system was reliable. However, should the bank experience any financial shock, whether due to internal or external factors, and if knowledge of that financial shock becomes public, then there is a risk that all depositors could request the return of their funds en masse. This phenomenon is known as a 'run' on the bank. A run was even riskier to early bankers because there was no concept of limited liability; if they failed then all their assets, not just bank stock but family goods, property, and land, were up for grabs.[34]

The success of the fractional reserve system in the UK is evident from the general lack of such bank-runs in modern times, although runs do remain a possibility. In September 2007 the first run on a British bank in 150 years occurred at Northern Rock, a casualty of the 2007/2008 financial crisis that was bailed out by the Bank of England.[35] Iconic photographs from the time show customers queuing outside the bank to withdraw funds – a familiar scene in the seventeenth and eighteenth centuries. While customers of modern British financial institutions can rely on bail outs from the Bank of England and compensation from the Financial Services Compensation Scheme, seventeenth- and eighteenth-century customers of financial institutions had no such recourse.

Customers of failed institutions could file a case of bankruptcy against the proprietors, but this could be a lengthy and costly process. Upon the petition of a creditor or group of creditors, stating that a bankrupt had failed to pay, the Lord Chancellor issued a commission of bankruptcy. Commissioners, usually individuals familiar with the bankrupt, were appointed to examine the facts and decide on how best to divide the estate and satisfy the creditors. Commissions of bankruptcy could be avoided if the bankrupt made a composition with their creditors, whereby remaining institutional funds are split between the customers who had not recovered their full deposited funds, offering each a certain amount per pound of their capital back. For example, if the composition was 3s 6d per pound and your deposit was £150 then you would receive £19 10s. Bankruptcy law prior to 1705 was particularly harsh and concerned solely with the plight of creditors, taking no account of the extenuating circumstances of the debtor. Bankrupts were treated as frauds and delinquents who had not only failed to meet their obligations but attempted to conceal assets. It was only post-1705 that a distinction was made between honest and dishonest bankrupts. Debtors could thereafter declare themselves bankrupt, offering up their estate to creditors but recouping a small percentage to rebuild their lives.[36] As will become evident, goldsmith bankers faced their fair share of bankruptcy proceedings.

The fractional reserve system stands in stark contrast with continental deposit or exchange banking, which retained a 100% reserve. Funds deposited in the bank remained in the bank, allowing individuals to withdraw or pay whenever required, or transfer between accounts up to the value of the funds deposited. Exchange banks were public banks, government sponsored and regulated, and were not, originally, note-issuing banks. Whilst continental exchange banks existed purely to facilitate and regulate creditor-debtor relationships, fractional reserve banking served to extend credit and create economic growth: 'Goldsmith-banking was dominated by transactions between customer and *banker* and not transactions between customer and counter party *facilitated by a banker*'.[37] Continental exchange banks therefore acted as clearing houses, but in London there was no state-sponsored central clearing bank. Instead, the goldsmith bankers developed a system of inter-banker clearing that relied on the banks participating in a network, accepting and clearing each other's notes, thereby enabling the flow of money between customers and counter parties.

Inter-banker clearing

Each goldsmith banker issued their own promissory notes, but for those notes to circulate easily and to be used to make payments or be cashed in, customers needed the notes to be accepted at any goldsmith bank and not just the bank that issued the note. Wider acceptance of the note increased its liquidity and therefore its attractiveness as a credit instrument. However, accepting the note of a rival created a negative balance. As the accepting banker had not issued the note, and its value did not come from a balance on their books, they recorded it as an overdraft account in the issuing banker's name. The other banker likewise accepted notes he had not issued. So, someone holding a note originally issued by banker A could cash it in with banker B. Banker B would then record the value of that note, along with any other of A's notes he had accepted, as an overdraft owed to him by A. Banker A would do likewise and record an overdraft owed to him by B. Then, at a given moment, the two bankers would reckon their accounts, leaving one banker in debit and the other in credit, and settle the final amount.[38]

The process of clearing has long been known to historians, but it was originally thought that one goldsmith banker facilitated this process for the others as a central clearing bank. In the 1930s R. D. Richards argued that Edward Backwell's bank, the Unicorn on Lombard Street, acted as a clearing bank for other bankers and as such was the 'indispensable precursor of the Bank of England'.[39] Similarly in the 1980s Eric Kerridge described Backwell's as a central clearing bank, and J. Keith Horsefield called Backwell a 'banker's banker'.[40] It was not until the 1990s that Stephen Quinn dismissed the argument that Backwell acted as a central clearing bank, arguing that it only appeared that way because Backwell's were the only ledgers of a goldsmith bank established prior to the 1670s to survive. Through greater analysis of Backwell's ledgers and the records of goldsmith banks established after the 1670s, Quinn demonstrated that bankers were not clearing with each other through Backwell but clearing 'bilaterally with Backwell' and each other – inter-banker clearing rather than central clearing.[41]

Inter-banker clearing occurred organically. At some point in the mid-seventeenth century goldsmith bankers started accepting the notes issued by other goldsmith bankers and holding accounts at other banks to facilitate acceptance. They also cleared bills and orders payable by other banks. The use of goldsmiths' notes increased as more bankers accepted each other's notes, and the public became confident that notes would be accepted at a variety of locations. It was therefore in a banker's interest to be part of the clearing network. If they refused the notes of fellow bankers then that banker would refuse their notes, and the credit network would be restricted. Without surviving ledgers, the exact frequency of clearing between banks or average amounts cleared is unknown. However, using Backwell's surviving ledgers to investigate clearing activities in 1670 between Backwell and three other goldsmith bankers, Quinn found that most notes were cleared within a few days, and over 90% were cleared within one week.[42] Additionally, Philip Winterbottom's analysis of goldsmith banker Edward Backwell's accounts for the year from 25 March 1671 to 25 March 1672 shows that accounts used by goldsmiths to bilaterally clear with Backwell were some of the most active on his books. On average, accounts saw 12.4 transactions per year, but the average amongst clearing accounts held by goldsmith bankers was much higher at 319.1 transactions. Whilst the average turnover of all accounts for the year was £2,606, the average for the clearing accounts was £74,908.[43] This suggests that clearing was a large and recurrent process.

Inter-banker clearing was not managed or overseen by a regulatory body but was self-regulatory. It was in the interest of the banker to clear their fellow banker's overdraft, as it was non-interest bearing and held no gain for them. The fact that the overdrafts were not interest bearing also meant there was no incentive in delaying the clearing process to build up a 'war chest of a competitor's notes' and cause a run on the competitor's bank.[44] This clearing system also made all of its participant bankers aware of money flows of their competitors, which on occasion enabled bankers to support each other against the risk of a run, promoting stability of the banking sector. The self-regulation of inter-banker clearing was also aided by the Goldsmiths' Company. Whilst the Company did not have regulatory powers over banking activities, it provided a sort of screening function as it restricted the number of new bankers entering the network through apprenticeship, which likewise ensured that those entering the network were familiar to their fellow bankers and reliable.[45] Despite their move into banking and, for many, away from making plate and jewellery, the Company remained a useful institution for goldsmith bankers.

Paper money?

Goldsmiths' notes, and the sophisticated clearing system that supported their circulation, have been described by some historians as representing the origins of paper money in England – a note could be passed from hand-to-hand and used to settle a payment, or clear a debt, in lieu of gold or silver. Jonchul Kim argues that the bearer clause gave the notes equivalence with money, they could be cashed on demand suggesting the 'notes were equivalent to gold that was safely kept in goldsmith's vaults', despite the fractional reserve breaking the direct link between notes and physical coin. Using notes, Kim argues, goldsmiths 'created credit out of thin air', backed as they were by only a fraction of real coin sitting in the vaults.[46]

However, Desan argues that goldsmiths' notes were not money in the way that later Bank of England paper notes became money. This was because the goldsmiths' notes were not universally accepted and were geographically limited. Whilst an individual could borrow in notes from a goldsmith banker and use those notes to make payments, they could not be certain that others would accept the notes and the government had no vested interest in accepting the notes as payment for taxes. Goldsmiths' notes could operate as credit locally amongst networks familiar with that particular banker, but when used as payment the notes would usually be cashed relatively quickly or transferred a limited number of times rather than circulating long term as trusted currency. The goldsmith's notes were, according to Desan, essentially 'a stand-in for specie that a goldsmith banker might or might not have on hand'.[47]

Whilst not fully functioning as paper money, the goldsmiths' use of notes and fractional reserve was innovative and expanded credit networks. Many of the goldsmiths' practices, and the wider use of bills and notes, were not sanctioned by common law but were necessary and practical for an increasingly commercial society. The use of such notes depended on trust and so the individuals issuing them were central to the system. Who some of those individuals were, the size of their banks, and the nature of their clientele are the subject of the following chapter.

Notes

1 Craig Muldrew, *The Economy of Obligation: The Culture of Credit and Social Relations in Early Modern England* (Basingstoke: Macmillan, 1988), pp. 6, 99–101.
2 Peter Temin and Hans-Joachim Voth, *Prometheus Shackled: Goldsmith Banks and England's Financial Revolution after 1700* (Oxford: Oxford University Press, 2013), p. 72; Dorothy Clark, 'A Restoration Goldsmith-Banking House: The Vine on Lombard Street', in *Essays in Modern English History: In Honour of Wilbur Cortez Abbott* (Cambridge, Massachusetts: Harvard University Press, 1971), pp. 3, 7; Youssef Cassis and Phillip L. Cottrell, *Private Banking in Europe: Rise, Retreat, and Resurgence* (Oxford: Oxford University Press, 2015), p. 33; David Mitchell, 'Innovation and the Transfer of Skill in the Goldsmiths' Trade in Restoration London', in David Mitchell (ed.), *Goldsmiths, Silversmiths and Bankers: Innovation and the Transfer of Skill, 1550 to 1750* (London: Alan Sutton Publishing, 1995), p. 5; Stephen Quinn, 'Banking before the Bank: London's Unregulated Goldsmith-bankers, 1660–1694' (unpublished thesis) University of Illinois (1994), p. 15.
3 Stephen Quinn, 'The Glorious Revolution's Effect on English Private Finance: A Microhistory, 1680–1705', *The Journal of Economic History* 61 (2001), pp. 602, 605; Stephen Quinn, 'Tallies or Reserves? Sir Francis Child's Balance between Capital Reserves and Extending Credit to the Crown, 1685–1695', *Business and Economic History* 23 (1994), p. 41; R.D. Richards, *The Early History of Banking in England* (London: Routledge, 2012 reprint), p. 31.

4 For the legal regulation and development of pawnbroking, see Warren Swain and Karen Fairweather, 'The Legal Regulation of Pawnbroking in England, a Brief History', in James Devenney and Mel Kenny (eds.), *Consumer Credit, Debt and Investment in Europe* (Cambridge: Cambridge University Press, 2012), pp. 142–59.

5 Christine Desan, *Making Money: Coin, Currency, and the Coming of Capitalism* (Oxford: Oxford University Press, 2014), pp. 114, 232–4, 237; Eric Kerridge, *Trade and Banking in Early Modern England* (Manchester: Manchester University Press, 1988), p. 85.

6 For example, Healey shows goldsmiths involved in illegal bullion smuggling operations in 1618–20: Simon Healey, 'Star Chamber and the Bullion Trade, 1618–20', in K.J. Kesselring and Natalie Mears (eds.), *Star Chamber Matters: An Early Modern Court and Its Records* (London: University of London Press, 2021), pp. 175–94. For the later bullion trade and a goldsmith's involvement in clipping, see Stephen Quinn, 'Gold, Silver, and the Glorious Revolution: Arbitrage between Bills of Exchange and Bullion', *The Economic History Review, New Series* 49 (1996), pp. 473–90.

7 Charles Richard Baker and Bruno Cohanier, 'The Emergence of Bills of Exchange in the Late Medieval and Early Modern Periods', *Accounting History* 30 (2025), p. 354.

8 C.D. Chandaman, *The English Public Revenue, 1660–1688* (Oxford: Oxford University Press, 1975), pp. 287–91.

9 Desan, *Making Money*, p. 249.

10 Quinn, 'Tallies or Reserves?', pp. 46, 49; Bruce G. Carruthers, *City of Capital: Politics and Markets in the English Financial Revolution* (Princeton: Princeton University Press, 1996), pp. 55, 61, 67.

11 Henry Roseveare, *The Financial Revolution 1660–1760* (London: Longman, 1991), p. 20.

12 Chandaman, *English Public Revenue*, p. 293.

13 R.D. Richards, 'Mr Pepys and the Goldsmith Bankers', *Economic History* (1933), pp. 506–12; Clark, 'Restoration Goldsmith-Banking House', pp. 6, 17–18; *The Diary of Samuel Pepys*, https://www.pepysdiary.com/, e.g. 18 June 1666. Also: Colvill 21 July 1665, 28 August 1665; Meynell 8 June 1665.

14 Aaron Graham, 'Military Contractors and the Money Markets, 1700–15', in Aaron Graham and Patrick Walsh (eds.), *The British Fiscal-Military States, 1660-c.1783* (Oxford: Oxford University Press, 2016), pp. 83–112.

15 Kerridge, *Trade and Banking*, pp. 39–40.

16 W.S. Holdsworth, *A History of English Law*, Vol. VIII (London: Methuen & Co, 1925), p. 129; James Steven Rogers, *The Early History of the Law of Bills and Notes: A Study of the Origins of Anglo-American Commercial Law* (Cambridge: Cambridge University Press, 1995), pp. 32–41.

17 Quinn, 'Banking before the Bank', pp. 34–36; Larry Neal, *The Rise of Financial Capitalism: International Capital Markets in the Age of Reason* (Cambridge: Cambridge University Press, 1990), pp. 5–7.

18 Holdswoth, *A History of English Law*, pp. 141–3.

19 Desan, *Making Money*, p. 395.

20 John Marius, *Advice Concerning Bills of Exchange* (London, 1651), pp. 8–10.

21 Rogers, *Early History,* pp. 102–15, 121–2; Marius, *Advice*, pp. 4–5.

22 The extent to which the common law adopted the law merchant or developed the law as it saw fit is debated by Rogers, *Early History*, Chapter 6; and J.H. Baker, 'The Law Merchant and the Common Law before 1700', *The Cambridge Law Journal* 38 (1979), pp. 925–32.

23 Rogers, *Early History,* pp. 126, 136, 172; Holdsworth, *A History of English Law*, pp. 142–3, 155–63; Jongchul Kim, 'How Modern Banking Originated: The London Goldsmith-Bankers' Institutionalisation of Trust', *Business History* 53 (2011), pp. 941, 943; Kerridge, *Trade and Banking*, p. 68.

24 Kerridge, *Trade and Banking*, pp. 42, 71; Holdsworth, *A History of English Law*, pp. 139–74; Kim, 'How Modern Banking Originated', p. 143.
25 Kerridge, *Trade and Banking*, pp. 41–3.
26 Quinn, 'Banking before the Bank'; Kim, 'How Modern Banking Originated', pp. 943–4.
27 Richards, *Early History*, p. 40; Rogers, *Early History*, pp. 119–20.
28 Frank T. Melton, 'Goldsmiths' Notes, 1654–1655', *Journal of the Society of Archivists* 6 (2009), pp. 30–1.
29 Quinn, 'Banking before the Bank', pp. 23, 47–8, 53–4.
30 *An Act for giving like remedy upon promissory notes, as is now used upon bills of exchange, and for the better payment of inland-bills of exchange*, 1704.
31 Kerridge, *Trade and Banking*, pp. 51–4.
32 J. Keith Horsefield, *British Monetary Experiments 1650–1710* (London: G. Bell and Sons, 1960), p. xiv; Kerridge, *Trade and Banking*, pp. 58–9.
33 Kim, 'How Modern Banking Originated', pp. 939–40; Desan, *Making Money*, p. 18; Edward W. Fuller and Warren Young, *A Finance Theory of the Business Cycle: Net Present Value and Fractional Reserve Banking* (London: Routledge, 2025), pp. 77–81.
34 Quinn, 'Tallies or Reserves?', p. 40.
35 Moshe Arye Milevsky, *The Day the King Defaulted: Financial Lessons from the Stop of the Exchequer in 1672* (Cham: Palgrave, 2017), p. 160.
36 W.J. Jones, 'The Foundations of English Bankruptcy: Statutes and Commissions in the Early Modern Period', *Transactions of the American Philosophical Society* 69 (1979), pp. 1–63, particularly 25–7, 29–30; Emily Kadens, 'The Pitkin Affair: A Study of Fraud in Early English Bankruptcy', *American Bankruptcy Law Journal* 84 (2010), p. 485; Michael Quilter, 'Daniel Defoe: Bankrupt and Bankruptcy Reformer', *The Journal of Legal History*, 25 (2004), pp. 53–73; Mabel Winter, *Banking, Projecting, and Politicking in Early Modern England: The Rise and Fall of Thompson and Company 1671–1678* (Cham: Palgrave Macmillan, 2022), pp. 159–64.
37 Stephen Quinn, 'Balances and Goldsmith-bankers: The Co-ordination and Control of Inter-banker Debt Clearing in Seventeenth-century London', in David Mitchell (ed.), *Goldsmiths, Silversmiths and Bankers: Innovation and the Transfer of Skill, 1550 to 1750* (Stroud: Alan Sutton Publishing, 1995), p. 75; Richards, *Early History*, p. 105.
38 Quinn, 'Balances and Goldsmith-bankers', pp. 53–76; Stephen Quinn, 'Goldsmith-Banking: Mutual Acceptance and Interbank Clearing in Restoration London', *Explorations in Economic History* 34 (1997), pp. 411–32.
39 Richards, *Early History*, pp. 30, 31, 211.
40 Kerridge, *Trade and Banking*, pp. 77, 80; J. Keith Horsefield, 'The "Stop of the Exchequer" Revisited', *The Economic History Review* 35 (1982), p. 525.
41 Quinn, 'Goldsmith-Banking', p. 413. Price hinted at inter-banker clearing in the 1890s, stating 'All the goldsmiths of that time kept accounts with Backwell's for clearing purposes, as they likewise did with Blanchard and Child and all other goldsmiths, were their books only in existence to prove it'. In F.G. Hilton Price, *A Handbook of London Bankers, with Some Account of Their Predecessors the Early Goldsmiths* (London: The Leadenhall Press, 1891), p. 5.
42 Quinn, 'Balances and Goldsmith-Bankers', p. 73.
43 Philip Winterbottom, 'Bank Clients and the Development of Personal Banking in London, 1672–1780' (unpublished thesis), Institute of Historical Research, University of London (2024), pp. 115, 117.
44 Quinn, 'Balances and Goldsmith-bankers', pp. 64, 60.
45 Quinn, 'Goldsmith-Banking', p. 424.
46 Kim, 'How Modern Banking Originated', pp. 944–5.
47 Desan, *Making Money*, p. 300.

Bibliography

Primary sources

An Act for giving like remedy upon promissory notes, as is now used upon bills of exchange, and for the better payment of inland-bills of exchange, 1704.
Marius, John, *Advice Concerning Bils of Exchange* (London, 1655).

Books, edited collections, and journal articles

Ashton, Robert, 'Revenue Farming under the Early Stuarts', *The Economic History Review* 8 (1956), pp. 310–22.
Baker, Charles Richard, and Bruno Cohanier, 'The Emergence of Bills of Exchange in the Late Medieval and Early Modern Periods', *Accounting History* 30 (2025), pp. 341–61.
Baker, J.H., 'The Law Merchant and the Common Law before 1700', *The Cambridge Law Journal* 38 (1979), pp. 925–32.
Carruthers, Bruce G., *City of Capital: Politics and Markets in the English Financial Revolution* (Princeton: Princeton University Press, 1996).
Cassis, Youssef and Phillip L. Cottrell, *Private Banking in Europe: Rise, Retreat, and Resurgence* (Oxford: Oxford University Press, 2015).
Chandaman, C.D., *The English Public Revenue, 1660–1688* (Oxford: Oxford University Press, 1975).
Clark, Dorothy, 'A Restoration Goldsmith-Banking House: The Vine on Lombard Street', in *Essays in Modern English History: In Honour of Wilbur Cortez Abbott* (Cambridge, Massachusetts: Harvard University Press, 1971).
Desan, Christine, *Making Money: Coin, Currency, and the Coming of Capitalism* (Oxford: Oxford University Press, 2014).
Fuller, Edward W., and Warren Young, *A Financial Theory of the Business Cycle: Net Present Value and Fractional Reserve Banking* (Oxford: Taylor & Francis, 2025).
Graham, Aaron, 'Military Contractors and the Money Markets, 1700–15', in Aaron Graham and Patrick Walsh (eds.), *The British Fiscal-Military States, 1660–c.1783* (Oxford: Oxford University Press, 2016), pp. 83–112.
Healey, Simon, 'Star Chamber and the Bullion Trade, 1618–20', in K.J. Kesselring and Natalie Mears (eds.), *Star Chamber Matters: An Early Modern Court and Its Records* (London: University of London Press, 2021), pp. 175–94.
Holdsworth, W.S., *A History of English Law*, Vol. VIII (London: Methuen & Co, 1925).
Horsefield, J. Keith, *British Monetary Experiments 1650–1710* (London: G. Bell and Sons, 1960).
Horsefield, J. Keith, 'The "Stop of the Exchequer" Revisited', *The Economic History Review* 35 (1982), pp. 511–28.
Jones, W.J. 'The Foundations of English Bankruptcy: Statutes and Commissions in the Early Modern Period', *Transactions of the American Philosophical Society* 69 (1979), pp. 1–63.
Kadens, Emily, 'The Pitkin Affair: A Study of Fraud in Early English Bankruptcy', *American Bankruptcy Law Journal* 84 (2010), pp. 483–570.

Kerridge, Eric, *Trade and Banking in Early Modern England* (Manchester: Manchester University Press, 1988).

Kim, Jongchul, 'How Modern Banking Originated: The London Goldsmith-Bankers' Institutionalisation of Trust', *Business History* 53 (2011), pp. 939–59.

Melton, Frank T., 'Goldsmith Notes, 1654–1655', *Journal of the Society of Archivists* 6 (1978), pp. 30–1.

Mitchell, David, '"Mr. Fowle Pray Pay the Washwoman": The Trade of a London Goldsmith-Banker, 1660–1692', *Business and Economic History* 23 (1994), pp. 27–38.

Mitchell, David, 'Innovation and the Transfer of Skill in the Goldsmiths' Trade in Restoration London', in David Mitchell (ed.), *Goldsmiths, Silversmiths and Bankers: Innovation and the Transfer of Skill, 1550 to 1750* (Stroud: Alan Sutton Publishing, 1995), pp. 5–22.

Muldrew, Craig, *The Economy of Obligation: The Culture of Credit and Social Relations in Early Modern England* (Basingstoke: Macmillan, 1988).

Neal, Larry, *The Rise of Financial Capitalism: International Capital Markets in the Age of Reason* (Cambridge: Cambridge University Press, 1990).

Price, F.G. Hilton, *A Handbook of London Bankers, with Some Account of Their Predecessors the Early Goldsmiths* (London: The Leadenhall Press, 1891).

Quilter, Michael, 'Daniel Defoe: Bankrupt and Bankruptcy Reformer', *The Journal of Legal History*, 25 (2004), pp. 53–73.

Quinn, Stephen, 'Banking before the Bank: London's Unregulated Goldsmith-Bankers, 1660–1694' (unpublished thesis) University of Illinois (1994).

Quinn, Stephen, 'Tallies or Reserves? Sir Francis Child's Balance between Capital Reserves and Extending Credit to the Crown, 1685–1695', *Business and Economic History* 23 (1994), pp. 39–51.

Quinn, Stephen, 'Balances and Goldsmith-Bankers: The Co-ordination and Control of Inter-banker Debt Clearing in Seventeenth-century London', in David Mitchell (ed.), *Goldsmiths, Silversmiths and Bankers: Innovation and the Transfer of Skill, 1550 to 1750* (Stroud: Alan Sutton Publishing, 1995), pp. 53–76.

Quinn, Stephen, 'Gold, Silver, and the Glorious Revolution: Arbitrage between Bills of Exchange and Bullion', *The Economic History Review*, New Series 49 (1996), pp. 473–90.

Quinn, Stephen, 'Goldsmith-Banking: Mutual Acceptance and Interbank Clearing in Restoration London', *Explorations in Economic History* 34 (1997), pp. 411–32.

Quinn, Stephen, 'The Glorious Revolution's Effect on English Private Finance: A Microhistory, 1680–1705', *The Journal of Economic History* 61 (2001), pp. 593–615.

Richards, R.D., 'Mr Pepys and the Goldsmith Bankers', *Economic History* 8 (1933), pp. 500–20.

Richards, R.D., *The Early History of Banking in England* (London: Routledge, 2012 reprint).

Rogers, James Steven, *The Early History of the Law of Bills and Notes: A Study of the Origins of Anglo-American Commercial Law* (Cambridge: Cambridge University Press, 1995).

Roseveare, Henry, *The Financial Revolution 1660–1760* (London: Longman, 1991).

Swain, Warren, and Karen Fairweather, 'The Legal Regulation of Pawnbroking in England, a Brief History', in James Devenney and Mel Kenny (eds.), *Consumer*

Credit, Debt and Investment in Europe (Cambridge: Cambridge University Press, 2012), pp. 142–59.

Temin, Peter and Hans-Joachim Voth, *Prometheus Shackled: Goldsmith Banks and England's Financial Revolution after 1700* (Oxford: Oxford University Press, 2013).

Winter, Mabel, *Banking Projecting and Politicking in Early Modern England: The Rise and Fall of Thompson and Company 1671–1678* (Cham: Palgrave Macmillan, 2022).

Winterbottom, Philip, 'Bank Clients and the Development of Personal Banking in London, 1672–1780' (unpublished thesis), Institute of Historical Research, University of London (2024).

3 Early goldsmith bankers

There are very few surviving business records of early goldsmith bankers, particularly those operating as financiers early in the seventeenth century. As such, the first part of this chapter uses court records and surviving business records to examine the practices of goldsmiths acting as financiers at the turn of the seventeenth century. The remainder of this chapter focusses on goldsmith bankers from the mid-seventeenth century onwards. It uses lists compiled by F. G. Hilton Price in the nineteenth century, which have been subsequently analysed and revised by modern historians, to identify goldsmith bankers operating across the later seventeenth and eighteenth centuries. Price used contemporary business directories and other (unidentified) sources in his possession to compile lists of goldsmiths keeping 'running cashes' in the years 1670, 1677, 1687, and 1700. The lists are probably incomplete, listing only those bankers who were operating in those specific years, meaning that banks which were established and failed in the intervening years do not appear.[1] This chapter focusses on the 1670 list which features 31 banks, subsequently corrected to 32 banks by Frank Melton (Table 3.1).[2] Using a combination of surviving business records and government records, it explores the relative size of these banks, as well as analysing their clientele in terms of occupation and location, and ends with a discussion of goldsmith bankers' wider social lives, investigating their complementary roles in the Goldsmiths' Company and local politics.

Early seventeenth-century goldsmiths as financiers

One of the best sources to locate financial activity by early goldsmiths is in court records when their activities fell foul of the law, particularly the laws against usury. For example, in the late sixteenth century, goldsmith and moneylender Christopher Wase was frequently accused of usury, which he disguised through various schemes. In one scheme, Wase would offer to loan money to a customer but would also make them buy an item, such as a piece of jewellery, for an inflated price to act as interest on the loan. Another method was to draw up a bond with the borrower, which would include a penalty

DOI: 10.4324/9781003627449-3

clause that provided Wase with interest on his loan to the customer and a legal veil to disguise it.[3] The 'interest' achieved in such transactions would often exceed the legal rate and both parties to the transaction could therefore end up in court. Another tactic was used by fellow goldsmith and moneylender Humphrey Bankes. In 1585 Edward Andrews approached Bankes seeking a loan of £20. Bankes said he did not have £20 but did have some plate worth 10s per ounce that he would let Andrews take on bond. Andrews could then sell the plate to raise the money he needed and repay Bankes later. Having taken out the bond for £20, Andrews then found himself unable to get more than 5s per ounce for the plate and accused Bankes of usury as the difference between the loan value and the sale of plate was 50%.[4] These early legal cases show how goldsmiths used their skills, in assaying and accessibility to plate and jewellery, to provide financial services and become recognised as money-lenders. Early goldsmith activities were probably more prolific than these few instances recorded in surviving legal records.

Aside from court cases, very few records of goldsmiths' early financial activity survive. One important exception are the surviving account books and personal papers of Sir William Herrick. Herrick was born in Leicestershire and apprenticed to his older brother and London goldsmith, Nicholas. In 1587 Herrick obtained his freedom of the Goldsmiths' Company and set up shop at the sign of the Rose in Cheapside. Herrick quickly rose to prominence, was elected to local political roles in London and as MP for Leicester from 1601, and served as a prime warden in the Goldsmith's Company. He obtained the position of jeweller to the king shortly after James I's accession to the throne in 1603 and in 1616 became a teller of the Exchequer, a receiver and recorder of money. As well as his shop and residence in London, Herrick bought the Leicestershire manor of Beaumanor in 1595. Upon his appointment as royal jeweller Herrick stopped practising as a working goldsmith, instead conducting private commissions and moneylending.[5]

G. E. Aylmer claimed that 'In the way in which he borrowed as well as lent, Herrick could be said to have anticipated later goldsmith bankers who kept "running cashes".'[6] In some ways this is true. Herrick offered many banking services that later goldsmiths became famous for, but Herrick's moneylending and banking activities were less formal and reserved for a very limited clientele. This is evident from his accounts, which record the amount paid or received but not whether they were upon a bond, or pawn, or deposited funds. Herrick's financial services were not separated from his household accounts, so loans, deposits, and dealings with bonds sit alongside transactions for personal rent, to tradesmen for household work, and for victuals and clothing.[7] However, Herrick's accounts and personal papers provide an overview of the kind of business he was conducting and the amounts involved.

One of Herrick's primary services was acting as a 'banker to country landowners' who needed money in London for the political term or social season.[8] As early as 1594 Herrick was collecting rents for Henry Hastings,

Earl of Huntingdon, a fellow Leicestrian, from his Somerset estate and transferring funds to the earl's wife.[9] Other titled customers using Herrick's services included the Earl of Dunbar, the Earl of Nottingham, and the Earl of Montgomery. A significant proportion of Herrick's business with the nobility concerned the private commissioning of plate and jewellery. He also provided loans, such as £1,000 to the Earl of Suffolk in 1607 at 10% interest and a £1,000 repayment from Lord Compton in 1611 which carried £56 interest.[10]

Herrick was also a pawnbroker. On 25 January 1602 Dame Margaret Stanhope did 'bargaine and sell' to Herrick two candlesticks and six silver plate trenchers, which sale would become void upon payment of £105 at Herrick's shop on 28 July 1603.[11] He also took deposits, receiving £30 from Lady Warburton in October 1611 'to keep for her till the last of this moneth'.[12] There is evidence amongst his papers of inland bills of exchange with a 'bearer' clause. In 1595 Rowland Brentforth instructed Herrick to 'pay to Captaine Jefford or the bearer heirof the som of fyftie pounds of good mony for yt ys for so much Received of him heare in Plymouth' on 10 September. Herrick clearly accepted as Thomas Ladbrooke signed the note in confirmation of receipt on 1 October.[13] Whether Brentforth also deposited money with Herrick for the purpose of transmitting funds is unclear. Alongside moneylending, Herrick also invested in trade, paying £12 10s in 1611 to Sir Thomas Smyth, treasurer of the Virginia Company.[14] By 1619 his investment in the Virginia Company had increased to £25.[15]

One way in which Herrick clearly pre-empted later goldsmiths was as a Crown lender, which was a significant reason for his downfall. Herrick's accounts and letters demonstrate that he lent large sums to the Crown and experienced frequent delays in repayment and non-payment. Many payments concerned his role as royal jeweller. For example, in 1607 the king owed Herrick £11,541 plus interest for jewellery alone.[16] As a teller of the Exchequer, Herrick was often called upon to meet shortfalls in Crown revenue, repaid later from money coming into the Exchequer. In 1617 Herrick, along with two other tellers, was asked to advance £5,000 to the king to pay Lord Aubigny. Together they advanced £3,500, which sums were to be repaid later 'upon their severall accompts' at the Exchequer. Herrick was ordered to furnish the remaining £1,500, receiving an order and privy seal for repayment. However, in March 1619 Herrick remained unpaid. A letter to Herrick on behalf of the Crown stated that 'our Treasury have disposed otherwise for our service all such monies as came into your hands'. Three years after lending the money, Herrick petitioned the king for relief, stating that 'the merchante strangers of whom yor peticioner borrowed the greatest parte of these moneys have called theire moneys out of yor peticioners hands to the greate danger of his whole estate'. The Crown agreed to repay the money and further recognised that Herrick's 'creditt ys much impayred in the cittye by reason that he ys an accomptant unto us'.[17] This episode shows Herrick borrowing from others in order to lend to the Crown, acting as a broker or transmitter of funds and not, as later goldsmiths, lending out customer deposits.

Over the following few years Herrick lent more to the Crown. In March 1620 he was owed £5,477 10s, which reduced to £5,037 6s 8d in April 1621 but then increased with another loan of £3,000 in May 1621, taking the debt to over £8,000.[18] Herrick left his positions as royal jeweller and teller of the Exchequer around 1623, most likely because of Crown defaults in payment. Herrick spent the last decades of his life in financial difficulties, having sold off land and property since the 1620s but maintaining his house at Beaumanor, and died in 1653. Herrick and the other earlier goldsmiths acted as moneylenders and offered financial services, but that was not how they were principally defined. They did not use customer deposits to make loans to others and did not operate a fractional reserve. It was not until the mid-seventeenth century that goldsmiths would fully evolve into bankers.

Mid-century bankers

Goldsmith bankers become more visible in records from the mid-seventeenth century. The earliest surviving goldsmiths' note is from around this time, and it is believed that inter-banker clearing began as more goldsmiths' notes were issued.[19] Goldsmith bankers in the second half of the seventeenth century are generally grouped into two separate camps based on location. Those with shops in the area around Lombard Street, near the Royal Exchange and from 1694 the Bank of England, are collectively referred to as the 'City' banks. Lombard Street, named after medieval Italian financiers from Lombardy who settled there, had long been a home to goldsmiths and financiers alike and was the economic heart of the City of London.[20] Goldsmiths with their shops in Fleet Street, the Strand, and Covent Garden are collectively referred to as the 'West End' banks. Over time these two groups developed distinct clientele. City banks were primarily engaged in providing mercantile credit and discounting bills and government tallies, and came to primarily serve merchants, city tradesmen, and the monarchy. West End banks acted more frequently as financial agents for the nobility, gentry, and professions, collecting rents, providing mortgages, and buying and selling stocks and shares. These were distinct groups with their own networks that rarely overlapped. It is possible that the groups had inter-banker clearing arrangements with one another, but this is not evident from the few surviving ledgers and records.[21] The rest of this chapter examines goldsmith bankers in the 1660s and 1670s (Table 3.1), providing, where possible, information on the size of their banks, their clientele, political roles, and other professional activity.

Of the 32 banks evident in 1670, 65.6% were City banks, 21.9% were West End banks, and a further 12.5% were at locations unknown. City banks appear to have significantly outnumbered West End banks. Source material in the form of ledgers or accounts survives for only three (9.4%) of these banks – the banks of Edward Backwell, Robert Blanchard and Francis Child, and Thomas Fowle – and these are incomplete. Backwell's ledgers, held in the NatWest

Table 3.1 Goldsmith Bankers Operating in 1670[22]

Bank	*Location*	*Goldsmith's Company*	*Politics*
Edward Backwell	City	Free 1651, Prime warden 1660–61	Alderman discharged 1660, treasurer Dunkirk garrison, MP 1673–83
Blanchard and Child	West End	Liveryman 1671, assistant 1688, prime warden 1690–91, master 1702	Child a Common Councillor 1682, alderman 1689 and knighted, Lord Mayor 1698–99. Royal jeweller 1689. MP 1702–8, 1710–13
John Collier	?		
John Colville	City	Free 1655, liveryman 1660, prime warden 1669	Churchwarden 1669 St Mary Woolchurch, Alderman sworn and discharged 1669
John East	West End		
Thomas Fowle	West End	Free 1660, prime warden 1687–88	Alderman 1686 and MP
John Harling	City		
Hinde and Kirwood	City		
Benjamin Hinton and Co	City		
James Hoare	City		
John Holmes	City		
Joseph and Nath Hornby	City		
John Lindsay	City		
Mawson and co	West End		
(Francis then) Isack Meynell	City		Francis an Alderman 1660–66
William Pinckney	West End		
John Portman	City	Free 1636	Common Councillor 1670–77
Thomas Rowe	City		
Robert Ryves	?		
George & John Snell	City	George free 1626/7, warden 1656, 1661, 1663	
Jeremiah Snow	City	Free 1649/50, liveryman 1660, prime warden 1679	Common Councillor 1673
Snow and Walton	West End		
Humphrey Stocks	City		
John Sweetaple	City	Free 1670, liveryman 1671, prime warden 1696	Common Councillor 1682, 1688–1701, Sheriff 1694
John Tassell	City		

(Continued)

Table 3.1 (Continued)

Bank	*Location*	*Goldsmith's Company*	*Politics*
Bernard Turner	City		
Sir George Viner	City		
Sir Robert Vyner	City	Free 1656, prime warden 1666	King's jeweller 1661, Knighted 1665, baronet and alderman 1666, high sheriff of London 1667, Lord Mayor 1674
John Warner	West End		
Robert Welstead	City	Free 1646, liveryman 1660	Common Councillor 1676
Gilbert Whitehall	?		
Thomas Williams	City		

Archives, are catalogued alphabetically and survive from ledger I to ledger S, from 1663 to 1671. Presumably there was a ledger A, so the records are incomplete but still represent the best set of surviving early bank accounts. The Child & Co records, also in the NatWest Archives, comprise customer ledgers from the 1660s onwards and balance books starting in the 1680s, with the bulk of the other records beginning in the eighteenth century.[23] Thomas Fowle's only surviving records are a 1660s Day Book and associated papers unearthed from Chancery Master's Exhibits by David Mitchell.[24] Lack of surviving sources is largely due to the relatively short lifespan of these banks. Of the 32 banks listed in 1670, 11 survived into 1687, and only four survived into 1700. Additionally, one of those four, the bank of Joseph Hornby, failed in 1701.[25] Not all banks suffered bankruptcy, some disappeared due to a lack of suitable heirs, retirement, and voluntary closure.[26] When banks closed or failed, records were often destroyed, leaving only traces of their activity, which render in-depth analysis in the form of balance sheets impossible.

Indirect sources, such as court cases and government documents, can also shed light on the banks. An important source in this regard is the Goldsmiths' Assignment Books (E 406) created after the Stop on the Exchequer in 1672, when the Crown ceased repayments of debts, which is the subject of the following chapter. These books provide limited information on some clients of ten banks – those of Vyner, Backwell, Whitehall, Lindsay, Portman, and Snell, and to a lesser extent of Rowe, Ryves, Snow, and Welstead. Ling-Fan Li's research demonstrates the utility of these records for prosopography, as the books record the name, profession, and location of goldsmith bankers' creditors affected by the Stop. Li's own analysis of these records focusses on the secondary market for government debt between 1677 and 1705.[27] This chapter instead uses the Assignment Books to investigate the original creditors of each goldsmith banker.[28] Richards argued that these sources could be used to fill the gaps left by non-extant bank ledgers.[29] However, whilst these records do provide a significant insight, they do not account for all the customers of these banks in the early 1670s and cannot be relied upon to give an accurate representation of the number of clients these banks had over the period they were in existence. What they do allow for is analysis of the recorded creditors by number, size of deposit, occupation, and location – a snapshot of the wider banking community.

Size of the banks

Whilst the Assignment Books do not account for all customers, they can give an idea of the bankers' size in relation to one another. The evidence suggests that the largest bank in the early 1670s was operated by Sir Robert Vyner, followed by Edward Backwell (Table 3.2). Vyner and Backwell were two of the most prominent goldsmith bankers of the period, acting as bankers to the Crown and government as well as numerous private individuals. They were both apprenticed to Sir Thomas Vyner in 1635 and 1646, respectively. Thomas Vyner was a successful goldsmith involved in financial activities, providing cash and credit to both the Commonwealth and Restoration governments, acting as a tax farmer, and was active in the bullion trade and coining at the Mint. He was also involved in politics, serving as alderman and sheriff of London in the 1640s, and knighted and elected Lord Mayor of London in the 1650s.[30] Vyner's blueprint for success was followed and exceeded by his apprentices, expanding his and their own businesses into fully fledged large-scale banks. Backwell set up his own business in the 1650s at the Unicorn on Lombard Street, having obtained his freedom from the Goldsmiths' Company in 1651. Robert Vyner became free of the Company in 1656 and joined his uncle and master Thomas in partnership at the Vine, fully taking over the business after his uncle's death in 1665.

Table 3.2 Amounts on Deposit with Ten Goldsmith Bankers[37]

Banker	*Amount on Deposit*	*Number of Creditors*	*Average Deposit (nearest £)*
Vyner	£398,750 15s 8d	905	£440
Backwell	£248,815 7s 11d	488	£510
Whitehall	£200,646 4s	433	£463
Lyndsay	£85,830 7s 8d	156	£550
Portman	£75,296 5s 3d	231	£326
Snow	£14,791 9s 4d	47	£315
Ryves	£13,338 9s	7	£1,905
Welstead	£9,585 17s 4d	21	£457
Snell	£7,011 3s 4d	42	£167
Rowe	£2,851 2s 6d	19	£150
	£1,056,917 4s 2d	2,349	

Sir Robert Vyner had over 900 creditors who collectively deposited just under £400,000 in his bank, which he then used to lend to the king via government tallies. The other bankers had significantly fewer recorded assignments than Vyner, which reflects Vyner's position as one of, if not the, principal lender to the Crown.[31] Vyner and Backwell were deeply involved in government finance, providing private loans to the Crown and taking on government contracts alongside their regular banking activities. In 1667 Vyner was owed £1,550,000 by the Crown from loans made to carry out the Second Anglo-Dutch War and loans made during the plague.[32] Both Vyner and Backwell were involved in tax farming in the 1660s.[33] Tax farming was the preserve of wealthy businessmen, usually acting in syndicates, who had the means to advance large sums of money in lieu of taxes which they would then collect at a later date, making a profit through the surplus of the amount collected over the value of their advance.[34] Backwell's services also extended to acting as a royal agent abroad to handle negotiations over sales, transfers of money, and the collection of dowries.[35] The extent of Vyner and Backwell's Crown lending, at rates in excess of the usury limit, meant they were well placed to offer attractive interest-bearing deposit accounts. A fragmentary account covering three weeks in September 1666 is all that survives of Vyner's ledgers, but it reveals that Vyner was dealing in significant amounts of money, having an average of £5,000 in hand at the end of each day.[36]

The Assignment Books only provide evidence of those holding deposit accounts at the banks at the time of the Stop, but Backwell's ledgers can be used to judge the extent to which the Assignment Books reflect the actual size of the banks and number of customers. Whilst Backwell's assignments in 1677 account for 488 customers holding deposit accounts at the time of the Stop in 1672, the ledger covering the period 25 March 1671 to 25 March 1672 details 1,899 customers. The difference between the two figures can in part be explained by taking a closer look at why customers used banks. As Philip Winterbottom has argued, different customers used bank accounts for different purposes. Of Backwell's 1,899 customers, just over half were using deposit accounts accruing interest, a quarter were using accounts similar to the modern current account, and the rest were used for a variety of purposes including borrowing, dealing with bills of exchange, property, accounts to facilitate the tax revenue, currency exchange, and clearing notes between goldsmith bankers.[38] The deposit accounts made up the fund used by Backwell to purchase and discount government tallies, and so those 900-plus account holders are the ones appearing in the assignments. The lower number can be accounted for by some customers having extracted their money earlier in the year, and others quickly extracting their money before the full effect of the Stop kicked in and Backwell stopped further payments.

The example of Backwell suggests that other banks could have been significantly larger than the number of customers evident in the Assignment Books suggests. Henry Roseveare used Backwell's ledgers from 1664 to 1672 to estimate the annual average amount Backwell had on deposit, which came to £420,000.[39] Using rough estimates of the size of the other goldsmith banks, largely in relation to the Assignment Books evidence, Roseveare argued that the largest goldsmith bankers (Vyner, Backwell, Colville, Meynell, Snow, Hornby, Snell, Portman, and Rowe) could have had £2 million collectively deposited with them in any year. This increased to a possible £3 million if other, smaller goldsmith banks were added into the equation. Without ledgers this is just an educated guess, but it does demonstrate the scale of goldsmith banking in the 1660s. It has been roughly estimated that the amount of gold and silver coin in circulation in England in the 1670s was about £12 million.[40] Using Roseveare's estimate, the amount held on deposit by goldsmiths, although not all in the form of coin, equalled about one-sixth or one-fifth of the amount of metallic money in circulation. Roseveare added, and it will be further explored in Chapter 5, that none of the eighteenth-century banking houses were of the same scale as either Backwell or Vyner, and that the scale of goldsmith banks 'attests to a well-established "banking habit" in the moneyed community' of Restoration London.[41]

The Assignment Books evidence concerns the larger, mostly City bankers who were predominantly bankers rather than working goldsmiths. Meanwhile, smaller goldsmith banking outlets, mostly located in the West End, took a longer transition into banking and continued to conduct a significant plate and jewellery trade. Two examples to judge the size of these banks can be found in surviving records. The first is Thomas Fowle, whose shop was on Fleet Street and whose daybook for the years 1664–67 provides evidence of 'the sale of plate and jewelry, bullion exchange, and the provision of financial services'. Evidence of financial services is limited as the purpose of many receipts is not identified. However, David Mitchell calculated Fowle's transactions for two six-month periods in 1664 and 1667. From September 1664 to March 1665 Fowle received £323 in loan repayments and redeemed pawns and gave out further loans (some against pawns) of £267. From September 1666 to March 1667, he received £953 and gave out a further £776 in loans. Fowle's business was clearly growing but his financial services were not in the same league as the larger City bankers, and most of his profit in the 1660s derived from the exchange of coin and the sale of plate and jewellery rather than from banking.[42]

Another Fleet Street banker with some surviving records was Robert Blanchard, who started banking at a similar time to Backwell. Blanchard's incomplete ledgers provide evidence of 115 customer accounts from January to December 1672, meaning his bank was significantly smaller than the top five goldsmith banks listed in the Assignment Books.[43] Blanchard's accounts were used mostly (72.4%) to draw notes from their account balance, termed by contemporaries a 'running cash', like a modern current account. The balance might be drawn on in a number of ways: to pay a named third party, like a cheque; to withdraw money for the customer's own use; and to pay for 'goldsmithing services'.[44] Neither Blanchard nor Fowle lent to the Crown, and neither offered interest-bearing deposit accounts. Their businesses served a different purpose to the City banks captured in the Assignment Books.

However, not all City banks were large Crown lenders offering interest-bearing deposits. No business records for the partnership of John Hinde and Thomas Kirwood survive, but insights can be gained from a series of legal disputes in the Court of Chancery in which they are described as 'goldsmiths or bankers' operating a shop in Cornhill.[45] Hinde and Kirwood were clearly successful goldsmiths as they also operated as tax farmers of the hearth tax in the 1660s before their bank partnership began.[46] The bank partnership commenced in 1671, although Kirwood was working as a goldsmith banker prior to this. Hinde and Kirwood did not pay interest on deposit accounts but offered overdrafts on which the customer would pay 'legall interest'. [47] Hinde and Kirwood's customers' deposits were used to discount bills of exchange, invest in mercantile companies like the East India Company, and later in construction projects and building works.[48] There are no references in the court cases to jewellery, plate, or pawn broking, and the extent to which they maintained their goldsmith trade is unclear. Hinde and Kirwood were not a large firm. A 1685 pamphlet, published after the death of Kirwood and occasioned by the bankruptcy of Hinde, mentions 150 creditors and amounts invested in real estate in the tens of thousands rather than the hundreds of thousands.[49] The example of Hinde and Kirwood suggests that many of the lesser-known City banks were much smaller ventures than the likes of Vyner and Backwell.

Clientele

Whilst the number of bank clientele and the amount on deposit were significant, it must be remembered that banks in the Restoration era catered only to the 'monied' community. Bank ledgers do not normally provide evidence of the address or occupation of customers. However, the Assignment Books did record this information for most of the depositors and can be used to assess their occupational status and geographical spread. In terms of occupation and social status, knights, baronets, and peers, along with gentlemen and those loosely described as 'esquire', made up the majority of depositors listed in the books. These are the wealthiest members of society, in possession of spare capital, and who might use a banker to collect rent for them and pay for services. Widows were also well represented. Historians have shown that widows were active in early modern financial markets, more so than married or unmarried women,[50] but the number of widows could also have been inflated as they inherited the deposits of deceased partners rather than creating their own accounts. Merchants and tradesmen also featured heavily in the clientele and appear to have been almost solely London based. Taking Vyner's depositors as an example, only one of the merchants

Table 3.3 Status/Occupation of the Customers of Ten Goldsmith Bankers by Percentage[52]

Gender	Occupation	*Vyner*	*Backwell*	*Whitehall*	*Lindsay*	*Portman*	*Snell*	*Welstead*	*Snow*	*Rowe*	*Ryves*
	Unknown	1	24	1	1	4	0	0	13	5	0
Female	Dame/Lady	1	1	1	1	2	0	0	0	0	14
	Spinster	4	2	5	1	4	5	0	4	0	0
	Widow	11	8	10	11	12	5	14	15	5	14
	Wife	1	0	0	0	0	2	0	0	0	0
Male	Knights, baronets, and peers	8	8	7	6	6	5	5	4	16	0
	Esquire	18	17	17	11	14	2	19	11	21	57
	Gentleman	21	15	21	23	13	16	24	21	11	14
	Professional	2	2	2	3	1	0	5	4	0	0
	Merchant	6	4	12	22	12	12	14	9	26	0
	Church	1	0	2	1	1	2	10	0	0	0
	Agricultural	1	0	0	0	1	2	0	0	0	0
	Victualling trades	5	4	4	7	4	9	0	2	5	0
	Building trade	2	1	2	1	1	2	0	0	0	0
	Cloth trade	7	4	9	7	10	16	0	11	0	0
	Other	9	8	7	8	17	21	10	6	11	0

and one tradesman, involved in the building trade, had an address outside of London, Middlesex, and the Home Counties. Merchants and tradesmen used banks to facilitate payments overseas and between one another via simple transfer in the ledgers. Banks allowed merchants and tradesmen to carry out large transactions without having to physically move money from one place to another, which was incredibly risky. Bank accounts were, therefore, concentrated in the hands of a minority of titled individuals and wealthy businessmen in this period (Table 3.3).[51]

The evidence also suggests that goldsmiths' customers more generally were confined to the London area (Graph 3.1). London and Middlesex together comprised between 53% and 85% of creditors of these banks, rising to between 60% and 90% when including the Home Counties. The dominance of London-based clients is expected, given the location of the banks and the area in which their notes circulated. Provincial customers were more likely to be country gentry redirecting their funds to London. For example, 79% of Vyner's depositors from outside London, Middlesex, and the Home Counties were titled, gentlemen, or esquires.

The clientele of Hinde and Kirwood are unidentifiable due to the lack of ledgers, but customers appearing against them in Chancery Court cases fit the stereotypical bank customer, as London residents and wealthy tradesmen. For example, Thomas Deane, William Wood, Christopher Rigault, and James Littleton were all London merchants, and John Ridges was a London skinner.[53] Hinde and Kirwood's business highlights the mercantile focus of City banks. They were described as having 'the Trust of receiving keepeinge & payinge greate sumes of money' and of 'usually receiving and paying the money of the merchants in the said City'.[54] The accounts of Thomas Deane from May

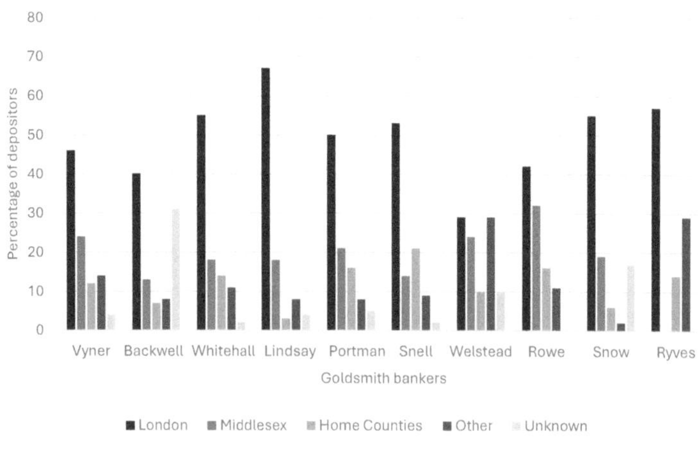

Graph 3.1 Location of the customers of ten goldsmith bankers.[68]

1671 to October 1673, submitted as evidence to the court, show Hinde and Kirwood facilitating payments to and from a variety of goldsmith banks, the scrivener bank of Clayton and Morris, and the bank of Thompson and Company, possibly settling bills of exchange and business with other merchants.[55] Hinde and Kirwood also discounted bills of exchange. London skinner Ridges complained that a bill he had discounted with them, and upon which he had constructed an elaborate chain of credit to facilitate his trade in Ireland, had been fraudulently used by Hinde and Kirwood, who were denying it had been settled and were trying to have Ridges arrested and fined.[56] This limited evidence suggests Hinde and Kirwood ran a typical City bank facilitating mercantile business in the London area.

The same geographical spread was probably true of West End banks, although there is less supporting evidence. Winterbottom has analysed Blanchard's creditors for the year 1672, identifying 79% of them by location. The majority of those identified (79.1%) were concentrated in London and the Home Counties.[57] Customers from further afield were the exception, not the norm.

In terms of gender, male depositors, over 80%, significantly outweigh female depositors in the Assignment Books (Table 3.4). Limited evidence for the smaller West End banks suggests a similar tale, with Blanchard's 1672 ledger revealing a similar gender divide.[59] In his analysis of goldsmiths' depositors in the Assignment Books, Carruthers found that the average size of deposit was higher for male customers (£493) than for female customers (£294).[60] Additionally, Winterbottom found that male clients of both Backwell and Blanchard in the 1672 ledgers were using their accounts for a wider range of activities than female clients, including to facilitate trading transactions and process bills of exchange alongside deposit accounts. The average number of transactions in female accounts was much lower than their male equivalents. Most women deposited in Backwell's bank to earn interest for investment purposes rather

Table 3.4 The Gender Divide of Customers at Ten Goldsmith Banks[58]

Goldsmith Banker	*Male Creditors*	*Percentage*	*Female Creditors*	*Percentage*	*Total*
Sir Robert Vyner	759	84	146	16	905
Edward Backwell	399	82	89	18	488
Gilbert Whitehall	360	83	73	17	433
John Portman	187	81	44	19	231
John Lindsay	136	87	20	13	156
Sir Jeremiah Snow	37	79	10	21	47
George Snell	38	91	4	9	42
Robert Welstead	18	86	3	14	21
Thomas Rowe	18	95	1	5	19
Robert Ryves	5	71	2	29	7
Total	1,957	83	392	17	2,349

than any other financial services. Meanwhile, at Blanchard's bank, over half of women's accounts were used primarily for 'commissioning, buying, selling or altering of jewellery or plate'.[61] These gender-based divisions are based on limited evidence but it does suggest that monied women engaged with banks to a different extent and for different purposes than men in the 1660s and 1670s.

Civic institutions and politics

For the goldsmith banker, social and political life went hand-in-hand with business success. Election to political roles demonstrated an individual's social standing and trustworthiness. Goldsmith bankers often sought election to positions within the Goldsmiths' Company and to political roles on the City of London's governing body. Some also became MPs. If a goldsmith became involved in state finance, lending on government tallies or providing personal Crown loans, then knighthoods, positions within the Treasury, and court roles also became available. These roles brought with them extra responsibilities but further enhanced the goldsmith's reputation and creditworthiness.[62]

The Goldsmiths' Company was controlled by a Court of Assistants, made up of four Wardens and 20 or more Assistants, under which was the livery, and then the general body of freemen. Election to the livery gave the goldsmith the right to vote in parliamentary elections amongst other benefits. Each year, two liverymen were elected as Renter Wardens, receiving or paying the Company rents, and having served in this role became eligible for election to the Court of Assistants. Moving up the ranks was a slow process based on seniority. However, goldsmiths active in wider City politics could skip the process, paying a fine of 100 marks to 'be excused from all offices in the Company save that of Upper Warden'. David Mitchell found that in the first half of the seventeenth century only three goldsmiths skipped the process, Richard Rogers, William Gibbs, and Sir William Herrick. In the second half of the century, when goldsmith bankers became fully established, 26 goldsmiths skipped the process, 16 of whom were goldsmith bankers.[63] Clearly this route to the top was sought after by these influential individuals and was beneficial to them for their reputation and business success.

Alongside Company roles, goldsmiths and goldsmith bankers commonly held positions at the Mint or were involved in the coinage. For example, goldsmith banker James Hoare was comptroller of the Mint in 1661, Surveyor of the Meltings and Clerk of the Irons in 1665, and Warden of the Mint from 1679 to 1682.[64] Additionally, in 1661 Backwell, Vyner, and Meynell were appointed to undertake the recoinage, turning Commonwealth coins into currency for the restored monarchy. Together the three goldsmith bankers made an advance of £100,000 to the Exchequer and the expense of coining was borne by the Crown. Each banker was allowed 5s 10d on each £100 in old money turned into the Mint. Vyner's profit from this scheme was £19,456, and the other two likely saw similar gains.[65]

Table 3.1 demonstrates that approximately a third of the goldsmith bankers featured in the list were involved in politics alongside their banking career. Involvement was mostly with the City of London's governing body, consisting of an annually elected common council, two annually elected sheriffs, an elite council of 26 aldermen elected for life, and the Lord Mayor elected each year out of the council of aldermen. Goldsmith bankers' election to these roles demonstrated their social standing in the London community. Of the three who became MPs, two became MPs later in the 1680s and 1690s; only Edward Backwell was an MP in the 1670s, elected in 1673 for Wendover.[66] Vyner was more deeply connected to the royal court, holding the additional role of the king's goldsmith from 1661 and, like his uncle before him, served as Lord Mayor of London in 1674.[67]

Vyner and Backwell were somewhat exceptional figures in both their political and financial domination of Restoration London. They obtained more political roles as their financial relationship with the Crown deepened and the size of their banks increased. Whilst political power clearly aided the expansion of their banks, it also brought with it significant risk. The fortunes of both Vyner and Backwell became tied up with the fortunes of Crown finance, which was notoriously unstable and which had caused the downfall of numerous financiers in the past. In 1672 Vyner, Backwell, and some of the other major goldsmith banks of the day would become the latest victims of the Crown's financial dealings in the Stop on the Exchequer, which is the subject of the following chapter.

Whilst political and financial power to some extent went hand-in-hand, the early history of the goldsmith bankers is dominated by Vyner, Backwell, and a few other big names for whom there is surviving source material. However, they were not necessarily typical of the sector as a whole. Whilst one-third of the 1670 list of goldsmith bankers were involved in politics or Crown finance, two-thirds were seemingly not. Lesser-known goldsmith bankers likely operated small- to medium-sized businesses that provided banking services for wealthy private individuals and did not cross the threshold into political space. This chapter demonstrates that surviving source material affects the stories we tell about goldsmith banking and the extent to which we can assess its wider impact on society and finance.

Notes

1 F.G. Hilton Price, *A Handbook of London Bankers, with Some Account of Their Predecessors the Early Goldsmiths* (London: The Leadenhall Press, 1891), 'Goldsmiths Keeping Running Cashes', pp. 182–5.

2 Frank T. Melton, *Sir Robert Clayton and the Origins of English Deposit Banking 1658–1685* (Cambridge: Cambridge University Press, 1986), pp. 236–42.

3 Norman Jones, *God and the Moneylenders: Usury Law in Early Modern England* (Oxford: Basil Blackwell, 1989), pp. 82, 123, 134.

4 TNA, REQ 2/167/26, Androwes v Bankes, 1585. See also REQ 2/169/34, REQ 2/170/34, REQ 2/170/35.

5 Paula Watson, 'Heyricke, Sir William (1562–1653)', *History of Parliament online* (Henceforth HoP), https://www.historyofparliamentonline.org/volume/1604–1629/member/heyricke-sir-william-1562–1653; G.E. Aylmer, 'Herrick [Heyricke], Sir William (bap. 1562, d. 1653)', *Oxford Dictionary of National Biography* (henceforth *ODNB*), https://doi.org/10.1093/ref:odnb/13076; Bodleian Libraries, MS.Eng.hist.c.477, 'Public and private business, vol. I', 1571–1616, f. 191.
6 Aylmer, 'Herrick'.
7 Leicestershire Record Office (henceforth LRO), DG9/2049, Herrick Manuscripts, Personal & estate account book.
8 Eric Kerridge, *Trade and Banking in Early Modern England* (Manchester: Manchester University Press, 1988), pp. 52–4.
9 Bodleian Libraries, MS.Eng.hist.c.477, 'Public and private business', f. 127.
10 Bodleian Libraries, MS.Eng.hist.c.479, 'Financial papers of Sir William Herrick, 1602–1623', f.109; LRO, DG9/2049, p. 92.
11 Bodleian Libraries, MS.Eng.hist.c.477, 'Public and private business', f. 178.
12 LRO, DG9/2049, p. 98.
13 Bodleian Libraries, MS.Eng.hist.c.477, 'Public and private business', f. 141.
14 LRO, DG9/2049, p. 91.
15 Susan Myra Kingsbury, *The Records of the Virginia Company of London* (Washington: Library of Congress, 1906), vol. III, pp. 84, 325. Investment was reduced again in 1620 to £12 10s – p. 338.
16 Bodleian Libraries, MS.Eng.hist.c.479, 'Financial papers', ff. 50–1.
17 Bodleian Libraries, MS.Eng.hist.c.479, 'Financial papers', ff.56–66, 74
18 Bodleian Libraries, MS.Eng.hist.c.479, 'Financial papers', ff. 77–80.
19 Stephen Quinn, 'Goldsmith-Banking: Mutual Acceptance and Interbank Clearing in Restoration London', *Explorations in Economic History* 34 (1997), pp. 411–32; Frank T. Melton, 'Goldsmith Notes, 1654–1655', *Journal of the Society of Archivists* 6 (April 1978), pp. 30–1.
20 F.G. Hilton Price, *The Signs of Old Lombard Street* (London: Leadenhall Press, 1902), pp. 1–7.
21 David Mitchell, 'Innovation and the Transfer of Skill in the Goldsmiths' Trade in Restoration London', in David Mitchell (ed.), *Goldsmiths, Silversmiths and Bankers: Innovation and the Transfer of Skill, 1550 to 1750* (Stroud: Alan Sutton Publishing, 1995), pp. 9–10; Kerridge, *Trade and Banking*, pp. 77–8; David Mitchell, '"Mr. Fowle Pray Pay the Washwoman": The Trade of a London Goldsmith-Banker, 1660–1692', *Business and Economic History* 23 (1994), p. 28; Stephen Quinn, 'Tallies or Reserves? Sir Francis Child's Balance Between Capital Reserves and Extending Credit to the Crown, 1685–1695', *Business and Economic History* 23 (1994), p. 49.
22 Price, *A Handbook of London Bankers*, pp. 182–5; Melton, *Sir Robert Clayton*, pp. 236–42; J.R. Woodhead, *The Rulers of London, 1660–1689: A Biographical Record of the Aldermen and Common Councilmen of the City of London* (London: London & Middlesex Archaeological Society, 1965); History of Parliament Online, https://www.historyofparliamentonline.org/
23 Summary: https://www.natwestgroup.com/heritage/companies/child-and-co.html.
24 Mitchell, 'Mr Fowle'.
25 Melton, *Sir Robert Clayton*, p. 234.
26 Gareth David Turner, 'English Banking in the Eighteenth Century: Bankers, Merchants and the Creation of the English Financial System' (unpublished thesis), Durham University (2015), p. 32.
27 Ling-Fan Li, 'The Stop of the Exchequer and the Secondary Market for English Sovereign Debt, 1677–1705', *The Journal of Economic History* 79 (2019), pp. 176–200. Many thanks to Ling-Fan Li for allowing me to use the data she

collected from TNA, E 406/16–26, Exchequer of Receipt: Assignments and Exchequer Bills, 'Goldsmiths' assignment book, Second series', 1676–1705.

28 Bruce Carruthers used the Assignment Books to analyse original creditors but did so as a collective rather than breaking down the creditors according to which goldsmith banker they held an account with: Bruce G. Carruthers, *City of Capital: Politics and Markets in the English Financial Revolution* (Princeton: Princeton University Press, 1996), pp. 61–9.

29 R.D. Richards, *The Early History of Banking in England* (London: Routledge, 2012 reprint), p. 79.

30 Dorothy Clark, 'A Restoration Goldsmith-Banking House: The Vine on Lombard Street', in *Essays in Modern English History: In Honour of Wilbur Cortez Abbott* Cambridge, Massachusetts: Harvard University Press (1971), pp. 3–47.

31 Clark, 'A Restoration Goldsmith-Banking House', pp. 3–47, particularly p. 6.

32 State Papers Online, SP 29/230 f.142, Statement of the services done to the State by Sir Rob. Vyner, 1667.

33 Clark, 'A Restoration Goldsmith-Banking House', pp. 6, 29; Lydia M. Marshall, 'The Levying of the Hearth Tax, 1662–1688', *The English Historical Review* 51 (1936), pp. 628–46.

34 Robert Ashton, 'Revenue Farming under the Early Stuarts', *The Economic History Review* 8 (1956), pp. 310–22.

35 Dorothy Clark, 'Edward Backwell as a Royal Agent', *The Economic History Review* 9 (1938), pp. 45–55; Clyde L. Grose, 'The Dunkirk Money, 1662', *The Journal of Modern History* 5 (1933), pp. 1–18.

36 G.E. Aylmer, 'Vyner [Viner], Sir Robert, baronet (1631–1688)', *ODNB*, https://doi.org/10.1093/ref:odnb/28318.

37 TNA, E 406, Goldsmiths' Assignment Books.

38 Philip Winterbottom, 'Bank Clients and the Development of Personal Banking in London, 1672–1780' (unpublished thesis), Institute of Historical Research, University of London (2024), pp. 64–6, 112–4; NatWest Group Archives NWGA EB/1/9.

39 Henry Roseveare, *The Financial Revolution 1660–1760* (London: Longman, 1991), p. 19.

40 N.J. Mayhew, 'Population, Money Supply, and the Velocity of Circulation in England, 1300–1700', *The Economic History Review* 48 (1995), p. 244.

41 Henry Roseveare, 'Government Financial Policy and the Money Market in Late Seventeenth Century England', in *Prodotto lordo e finanza pubblica* (Prato: Instituto Internazionale di Storia Economica, 1988), p. 732.

42 Mitchell, 'Mr Fowle', pp. 29–32. For more on Fowle's later business, see Chapter 5.

43 Winterbottom, 'Bank Clients', pp. 64 fn.29, 66; NatWest Group Archives NWGA CH/194/1–4, 6.

44 Winterbottom, 'Bank Clients', p. 119.

45 TNA, C 10/183/64, Ridges v Hinde, 1677; C 8/214/54 Kirwood v Deane, 1677; C 8/217/41 Kirwood and Hinde v Wood, 1679; C 10/139/56, Littleton v Hinde and Kirwood, 1679; C 8/258/46, Hinde and Kirwood v Deane, 1681.

46 Profits from tax farming caused later legal disputes: TNA, C 10/142/39 Hind v Perry 1681, C 10/484/91 Hinde v Dashwood 1683.

47 TNA, C 8/214/54 Kirwood and Hinde v Deane, 1677; TNA, C 8/217/41 Kirwood and Hinde v Wood. Court cases record partnership as beginning in 1671, but Price records them as partners in his 1670 list of goldsmith bankers.

48 British Library, IOR/L/AG/1/1/6/f.473(5), Thomas Kyrwood and John Hinde, Bond Holder 1673–75; IOR/L/AG/1/1/6/ff.495,527(2), Thomas Kirwood and John Hinde, personal account 1673–75; IOR/L/AG/1/1/7/f.52, Thomas Kirwood and John Hinde, Personal account 1676–78; *The Case of John Hinde Goldsmith with his Creditors justly stated Giving an Account to the World of the occasion of his*

Failing, his fair Proposals, and the Justness and Honesty of his Designs to all his Creditors (London, 1685).
49 *Case of John Hinde*, p. 12.
50 For example, B.A. Holderness, 'Widows in Pre-Industrial Society: An Essay Upon Their Economic Functions', in R.M. Smith (ed.) *Land, Kinship and Life-Cycle* (Cambridge: Cambridge University Press, 1984), pp. 423–42; Amy Louise Erickson, *Women and Property in Early Modern England* (London: Routledge, 1993), part 4.
51 Craig Muldrew, '"Hard Food for Midas": Cash and Its Social Value in Early Modern England', *Past & Present* 170 (2001), pp. 92–3.
52 TNA, E 406, Goldsmiths' Assignment Books.
53 TNA, C 8/214/54 Kirwood v Deane, 1677; C 8/258/46, Hinde v Deane; C 8/217/41, Kirwood and Hinde v Wood, 1679; C 7/288/36, Rigault v Hinde, 1685; C 10/139/56, Littleton v Hinde and Kirwood, 1679; C 10/183/64, Ridges v Hinde, 1677.
54 TNA, C 8/214/54 Kirwood v Deane, 1677; C 8/217/41 Kirwood and Hinde v Wood, 1679.
55 TNA, C 8/214/54 Kirwood v Deane, 1677. Goldsmith bankers mentioned include Thomas Rowe, John Lindsay, George Snell, Jeremy Snow, Isaac Meynell, Benjamin Hinton, Robert Welstead, and John Portman.
56 TNA, C 10/183/64, Ridges v Hinde, 1677.
57 Winterbottom, 'Bank Clients', p. 71.
58 TNA, E 406, Goldsmiths' Assignment Books.
59 Winterbottom, 'Bank Clients', p. 67.
60 Carruthers, *City of Capital*, p. 66.
61 Winterbottom, 'Bank Clients', pp. 67, 111–2, 120–1.
62 Perry Gauci, *The London Private Banker: A Social History, 1660–1825* (Oxford: Oxford University Press, 2025), pp. 26, 8, 137; Mabel Winter, *Banking Projecting and Politicking in Early Modern England: The Rise and Fall of Thompson and Company 1671–1678* (Cham: Palgrave Macmillan, 2022), pp. 17–21,181–205.
63 David Mitchell, *The Wider Goldsmiths' Trade in Elizabethan and Stuart London* (London: Ad Ilissum, 2024), pp. 32–9.
64 F.G. Hilton Price, 'Some Notes of the Early Goldsmiths and Bankers', *Transactions of the London and Middlesex Archaeological Society*, Vol. VI (London, 1881), p. 277; F.G. Hilton Price, *The Marygold by Temple Bar* (London: Bernard Quaritch, 1902), p. xxxi.
65 Clark, 'A Restoration Goldsmith-Banking House', pp. 19–20.
66 Leonard Naylor and Geoffrey Jaggar, 'Backwell, Edward (c.1618–83)', *HoP* https://www.historyofparliamentonline.org/volume/1660–1690/member/backwell-edward-1618–83.
67 Aylmer, 'Vyner', *ODNB*; Clark, 'A Restoration Goldsmith-Banking House', p. 41.
68 Aylmer, 'Vyner', *ODNB*; Clark, 'A Restoration Goldsmith-Banking House', p. 41.

Bibliography

Primary sources

Bodleian Libraries, MS.Eng.hist.c.477, 'Public and private business, vol. I', 1571–1616.
Bodleian Libraries, MS.Eng.hist.c.479, Financial papers of Sir William Herrick, 1602–1623.
British Library, IOR/L/AG/1/1/6/f.473(5), Thomas Kyrwood and John Hinde, Bond Holder 1673–75.

British Library, IOR/L/AG/1/1/6/ff.495,527(2), Thomas Kirwood and John Hinde, personal account 1673–75.
British Library, IOR/L/AG/1/1/7/f.52, Thomas Kirwood and John Hinde, Personal account 1676–78.
The Case of John Hinde Goldsmith with his Creditors justly stated Giving an Account to the World of the occasion of his Failing, his fair Proposals, and the Justness and Honesty of his Designs to all his Creditors (London, 1685).
Leicestershire Record Office, DG9/2049, Herrick Manuscripts, Personal & estate account book.
State Papers Online, SP 29/230 f.142, Statement of the services done to the State by Sir Rob. Vyner, 1667.
TNA, E 406/16–26, Exchequer of Receipt: Assignments and Exchequer Bills, 'Goldsmiths' assignment book, Second series', 1676–1705.
TNA, REQ 2/167/26, Androwes v Bankes, 1585.
TNA, REQ 2/169/34, Andrews v Bankes, 1586.
TNA, REQ 2/170/34, Androwes v Clarke, 1588.
TNA, REQ 2/170/35, Androwes v Banckes, 1599.
TNA, C 10/142/39 Hind v Perry 1681.
TNA, C 10/484/91 Hinde v Dashwood 1683.
TNA, C 8/214/54 Kirwood v Deane, 1677.
TNA, C 8/217/41 Kirwood and Hinde v Wood, 1679.
TNA, C 10/139/56, Littleton v Hinde and Kirwood, 1679.
TNA, C 10/183/64, Ridges v Hinde, 1677.
TNA, C 7/288/36, Rigault v Hinde, 1685.
TNA, C 8/258/46, Hinde v Deane, 1681.

Books, edited collections, and journal articles

Ashton, Robert, 'Revenue Farming under the Early Stuarts', *The Economic History Review* 8 (1956), pp. 310–22.
Carruthers, Bruce G. *City of Capital: Politics and Markets in the English Financial Revolution* (Princeton: Princeton University Press, 1996).
Clark, Dorothy, 'Edward Backwell as a Royal Agent', *The Economic History Review* 9 (1938), pp. 45–55.
Clark, Dorothy, 'A Restoration Goldsmith-Banking House: The Vine on Lombard Street', in *Essays in Modern English History: In Honour of Wilbur Cortez Abbott* Cambridge, Massachusetts: Harvard University Press (1971), pp. 3–47.
Erickson, Amy Louise, *Women and Property in Early Modern England* (London: Routledge, 1993).
Gauci, Perry, *The London Private Banker: A Social History, 1660–1825* (Oxford, Oxford University Press, 2025).
Grose, Clyde L., 'The Dunkirk Money, 1662', *The Journal of Modern History* 5 (1933), pp. 1–18.
Holderness, B.A., 'Widows in Pre-Industrial Society: An Essay upon Their Economic Functions', in R.M. Smith (ed.), *Land, Kinship and Life-Cycle* (Cambridge: Cambridge University Press, 1984), pp. 423–42.
Jones, Norman, *God and the Moneylenders: Usury Law in Early Modern England* (Oxford: Basil Blackwell, 1989).

Kerridge, Eric, *Trade and Banking in Early Modern England* (Manchester: Manchester University Press, 1988).

Kingsbury, Susan Myra, *The Records of the Virginia Company of London*, vol. 3 (Washington: Library of Congress, 1906).

Li, Ling-Fan, 'The Stop of the Exchequer and the Secondary Market for English Sovereign Debt, 1677–1705', *The Journal of Economic History* 79 (2019), pp. 176–200.

Marshall, Lydia M., 'The Levying of the Hearth Tax, 1662–1688', *The English Historical Review* 51 (1936), pp. 628–46.

Mayhew, N.J., 'Population, Money Supply, and the Velocity of Circulation in England, 1300–1700', *The Economic History Review* 48 (1995), pp. 238–57.

Melton, Frank T., *Sir Robert Clayton and the Origins of English Deposit Banking 1658–1685* (Cambridge: Cambridge University Press, 1986).

Melton, Frank T., 'Goldsmith Notes, 1654–1655', *Journal of the Society of Archivists* 6 (April 1978), pp. 30–1.

Mitchell, David, '"Mr. Fowle Pray Pay the Washwoman": The Trade of a London Goldsmith-Banker, 1660–1692', *Business and Economic History* 23 (1994), pp. 27–38.

Mitchell, David, 'Innovation and the Transfer of Skill in the Goldsmiths' Trade in Restoration London', in David Mitchell (ed.), *Goldsmiths, Silversmiths and Bankers: Innovation and the Transfer of Skill, 1550 to 1750* (Stroud: Alan Sutton Publishing, 1995).

Mitchell, David, *The Wider Goldsmiths' Trade in Elizabethan and Stuart London* (London: Ad Ilissum, 2024).

Muldrew, Craig, '"Hard Food for Midas": Cash and Its Social Value in Early Modern England', *Past & Present* (2001), pp. 78–120.

Price, F.G. Hilton, 'Some Notes of the Early Goldsmiths and Bankers', *Transactions of the London and Middlesex Archaeological Society*, Vol. VI (London, 1881), pp. 255–81.

Price, F.G. Hilton, *Handbook of London Bankers, with Some Account of Their Predecessors the Early Goldsmiths* (London: The Leadenhall Press, 1891).

Price, F.G. Hilton, *The Signs of Old Lombard Street* (London: Leadenhall Press, 1902).

Price, F.G. Hilton, *The Marygold by Temple Bar* (London: Bernard Quaritch, 1902).

Quinn, Stephen, 'Tallies or Reserves? Sir Francis Child's Balance between Capital Reserves and Extending Credit to the Crown, 1685–1695', *Business and Economic History* 23 (1994), pp. 39–51.

Quinn, Stephen, 'Goldsmith-Banking: Mutual Acceptance and Interbank Clearing in Restoration London', *Explorations in Economic History*, No. 34, (1997), pp. 411–32.

Richards, R.D., 'Mr Pepys and the Goldsmith Bankers', *Economic History* (1933), volume 2, pp. 500–520.

Richards, R.D., *The Early History of Banking in England* (London: Routledge, 2012 reprint).

Roseveare, Henry, 'Government Financial Policy and the Money Market in Late Seventeenth Century England', in *Prodotto lordo e finanza pubblica* (Prato: Instituto Internazionale di Storia Economica, 1988), edited by Annalisa Guarducci pp. 703–35.

Roseveare, Henry, *The Financial Revolution 1660–1760* (London: Longman, 1991).

Turner, Gareth David, 'English Banking in the Eighteenth Century: Bankers, Merchants and the Creation of the English Financial System' (unpublished thesis), Durham University (2015).
Winter, Mabel, *Banking Projecting and Politicking in Early Modern England: The Rise and Fall of Thompson and Company 1671–1678* (Cham: Palgrave Macmillan, 2022).
Winterbottom, Philip, 'Bank Clients and the Development of Personal Banking in London, 1672–1780' (unpublished thesis), Institute of Historical Research, University of London (2024).

Online databases

Oxford Dictionary of National Biography, https://www.oxforddnb.com/
History of Parliament Online, https://www.historyofparliamentonline.org/

4 Goldsmith banking and the 1672 Stop on the Exchequer

In January 1672 Charles II publicly announced that because 'His Revenues were so anticipated and engaged' he was 'to cause a Stop to be made of the payment of any Moneys, now being, or to be brought into His Exchequer'.[1] Intended at first to be a temporary stop lasting one year, this event was to drag on for decades, causing public scandal. The stop of payments particularly affected one financial instrument, the Treasury order, which since 1665 had become an important tool of administering government debt. As major Crown financiers, certain goldsmith bankers became heavily entangled in the Treasury order system. Although a larger number may have dealt in Treasury orders, there are 13 goldsmith bankers, all operating 'City' banks, who definitely dealt in the orders and who were heavily affected by the Stop on the Exchequer, as is evident from documents drawn up in response to the Stop. Therefore, 1672 marked a turning point in the careers of some of the most prominent bankers of the day. This chapter tells the story of the goldsmith bankers' involvement with Treasury orders and the Stop on the Exchequer.

Government finance

The Stop on the Exchequer was a consequence of how the English Crown funded itself. Monarchs were expected to fund their own household as well as justice and defence of the realm. Money was to be raised from the Crown estates, while Parliament levied supplementary taxes on the population for extraordinary expenditure, such as warfare. Monarchs had also long been private borrowers, taking up loans from domestic or foreign financiers to plug the gaps in their finances.[2] At the Restoration in 1660 it was recognised that rents from the Crown estates alone would not be sufficient, and so Charles II was granted taxes from the ordinary revenue – customs, excise, and hearth taxes – intended to provide him with a fund of £1.2 million.

For early modern monarchs, the problem with taxes was that they were paid in dribs and drabs throughout the year and did not correspond with the immediate needs of spending. This was particularly the case when funding war: taxes could be raised to meet costs, but the money would not be available

DOI: 10.4324/9781003627449-4

for months or years and there was often a shortfall between the estimated and actual revenue. This was true of both the ordinary revenue and supplementary direct taxes levied by parliamentary grants.[3] Additionally, Charles II began his reign with significant debts inherited from his father and the Commonwealth government, and Crown spending nearly always exceeded income, meaning the deficit kept climbing.[4] Between 1660 and 1671, average annual expenditure was over £1.5 million, clearly outstripping the funds provided.[5] The deficit was regularly plugged by loans.

In the 1660s the government primarily used short-term loans that accrued interest, matured regularly, and compounded. Rather than solving the underlying problem, the loans were adding to the deficit. In the early 1660s debt repayments made up 4.3% of Crown expenditure, but by the early 1670s had increased to 31% of expenditure.[6] Loans to the Crown primarily came from mercantile companies, the City of London, and prominent individual financiers, such as the goldsmith bankers, and were secured on various branches of the future tax revenue.[7] Loans to the monarch were not subject to the laws on maximum interest rates. So, whilst individuals seeking loans from financiers would pay 6%, the Crown would often pay up to and over 10% interest.

One of the most important sources of loans was tax farming. Because taxes were not immediately available, the collection of taxes was farmed out to a syndicate of financiers who would advance an agreed amount of money, in lump sums and regular monthly instalments, and then collect the taxes themselves as they became due. Any amount collected over the advance paid to the government was theirs as profit. Customs farmers were wealthy individuals, and they often made private loans to the Crown or accepted more tallies than the amount advanced, thus creating an overdraft.[8] Tax farming regulated the amount of money coming in and could be further utilised as a source of credit. This was achieved through the tally system.

From tallies to Treasury orders

Government tallies, used by the Treasury to make payments on the security of future revenue, were adapted in the mid-seventeenth century to create the Treasury order, the instrument that was key to the 1672 Stop. Treasury orders followed a similar process to tallies (see Chapter 2) but could also be used to raise loans directly from the public and, importantly, accrued interest. In this extension of the system, the lender agreed to loan money to government and received a tally as receipt. The tally was accompanied with a note from the Exchequer (the order), which recorded the amount along with the interest due, and specified that repayment would be made at a future date when the funds from an identified revenue stream became available. The addition of interest meant that tallies no longer represented a simple debt but cost the Crown money to borrow in anticipation of taxes.[9]

Sir George Downing, the brains behind the Treasury order scheme, wanted to reduce both the Crown's dependence on the goldsmith bankers and the amount the Crown had to pay in interest on loans. Downing had held numerous political offices during the Commonwealth under Oliver Cromwell and survived the Restoration of the monarchy, being knighted in 1660. Importantly, Downing had been an envoy to The Hague from 1657 and became well versed in Dutch economic policies and state finance, which the English so envied.[10] Throughout the seventeenth century the Dutch state could borrow money at 4%, much less than the 10% or more that the English Crown was forced to pay, normally to the goldsmith bankers.[11]

Downing advertised the benefits of his scheme, 'both for the Lender and for the King', in a pamphlet entitled *A State of the Case, between Furnishing His Majesty with Money* (1665). For the lender, the loan was secure, accessible, and assignable. For the king, the loan benefitted from being 'first hand' – not having to 'pay a double Interest' by going through financiers such as the goldsmith bankers – and it would 'raise the Credit of his Exchequer'.[12] Downing's scheme would increase the perceived security of lending to the Crown whilst lowering the interest rates individuals would accept for these loans, thus bringing England in line with the efficiency and cheapness of Dutch state lending. Instead of creditors depositing their money with goldsmiths at 6% interest and then goldsmiths using that deposited money to make loans to the Crown at 10%, Downing's system intended to cut out the middleman and have creditors simply loan money directly to the government at 6%, thus reducing the cost of government borrowing and, through steady and ordered repayments, increasing trust in lending to the Crown.

The Treasury order was a necessary innovation because in 1665 England faced a credit shortage due to the Second Anglo-Dutch War and financial difficulties brought about by plague. The King desperately needed funds, but the financiers and goldsmith bankers refused to provide further loans. On 31 October 1665 parliament passed the Additional Aid Act using an assessment which would be paid within two years to provide £1.25 million to fund the war effort. An assessment was essentially a land tax, a form of taxation developed in 1645 which calculated a levy through a monthly assessment of each county, 'which in turn re-distributed the burden amongst their principal men of property'.[13] The Additional Aid Act allowed for this tax to be anticipated through Treasury orders and added extra security for repayment. The money received had to be used for the war effort and could not be redirected for other uses by the monarch, and each order was to be numbered and repaid sequentially as and when the corresponding revenue was collected, preventing certain loans being paid earlier than others due to political preferment. As revenue funds came in, the order numbers due for repayment were announced in the *London Gazette* and, as Pepys noted, a list was also pasted on the door of the Exchequer.[14] The fairness of the system, security of repayment, and assignability of Treasury orders were designed to offer an incentive to those with money to advance it to government and accept 6% interest, a much lower amount than the Crown paid for other loans.

The orders were also given greater liquidity, as they were made legally transferable or assignable: the original holder of debt could transfer or sell it to another person, who would be legally entitled to collect the money from the Exchequer once the order became due. The liquidity of the orders was restricted though as they could not be cashed in immediately for money but had to wait their turn for repayment from a specified fund. Whilst tallies had previously been transferred to new holders, it was done informally without legal backing. Legal assignability was therefore intended to add further appeal to these financial instruments.

The goldsmith bankers enter the story

Despite Downing's efforts, goldsmith bankers played a key role in the success and downfall of Treasury orders. Goldsmiths entered the story through the transferability, or assignability, of Treasury orders. Those in receipt of Treasury orders, particularly government departments and those receiving them for goods and services proffered to the government, would often require or prefer the ready money before it matured. Even those purchasing Treasury orders as loans might want or need their money before it became due and decide to assign it to a third party for a payout. Downing envisaged the growth of a secondary market for these orders, passing from hand-to-hand to 'daily accommodate' transactions.[15] But the liquidity of Treasury orders was limited. To assign a Treasury order it had to be recorded in the Treasury books at the Exchequer, which was laborious. The act of physical assignment meant they were far less liquid than goldsmiths' notes.[16]

Goldsmith bankers dealt in Treasury orders because they could make a profit by discounting them. Like bills of exchange, bankers would offer immediate payment but of an amount lower than the face value of the order. When the order became due the banker received both face value and the interest accrued. Other individuals also discounted orders, but it was the goldsmiths who dominated the limited secondary market for Treasury orders and who remained crucial middlemen in Crown finances.[17]

The money the bankers used for purchasing, or discounting, Treasury orders was the pool of funds created by their clients' deposits in the fractional reserve system. The goldsmiths were the direct creditors, and their depositors were indirect creditors. What this meant was that clients' deposits were being held in the form of government debt. As Treasury orders came up for payment, its face value plus interest would go back into the bank, thus providing profit from which the bankers could pay interest on deposits, further invest, or provide loans. The extent to which depositors were aware of how their money was being used is unclear. Roseveare argued that following the 1672 Stop depositors argued in legal cases that their deposit had been made for convenience and 'they had no intention that the bankers should re-invest their funds in loans to the Crown'. However, the bankers' countered this by arguing that their involvement in government debt was common knowledge, as was the fact that government debt paid for interest rates on deposits – a key attraction for customers.[18] The fact that customers conducted a run on the bank upon hearing rumours of government default is further suggestive that they were aware of how their money was being used.

The fiduciary order

Whilst the money held in Treasury orders was seemingly quite safe, secured against specific and expected revenue streams, there was a major risk within the system: it depended on the continued management and cooperation of the Exchequer and the Crown. This risk came to the fore in 1667 when the Exchequer issued a variant on the Treasury order known as fiduciary orders. Whereas Treasury orders represented an actual transaction, whereby a lender or creditor made payment or provided goods, the fiduciary orders represented a fictitious payment. They were used for departmental spending. A departmental treasurer was given a fiduciary order in lieu of money, which was repaid later from a stream of revenue, and had to use those orders to raise money to conduct their business. Like Treasury orders, these orders were also numbered and due to be repaid sequentially. The treasurer could either try to use them for payments, giving them to suppliers; or they could utilise the secondary market and the services of a financier or goldsmith banker, using the order as security for a loan or have it discounted. Initially fiduciary orders were issued against specific revenue streams, such as the 1667 Additional Aid Act and the customs, excise, and hearth taxes, but then they began to be issued against the revenue in general – so repayment would be made from any available revenue at the specified date of repayment rather than being assigned to a specific revenue stream. This kind of borrowing immediately opens the possibility of overspending. If the amounts borrowed are tied to a defined amount of future revenue from a specific stream, then it restricts the government from borrowing beyond that amount. However, when payments are secured on the general revenue there is no consideration of the actual amounts that will be received in future taxes; it is simply borrowing the required sums for present spending and trusting that some undefined future revenue will be available to repay it.[19] As was the case with Treasury orders, the majority of fiduciary orders ended up in the hands of certain goldsmith bankers.

Further problems in Crown finance

Fiduciary orders were used to facilitate increased spending during the second half of the 1660s, when Crown finances took a significant hit due to the Second Anglo-Dutch War and decreases in revenue collection due to plague and the Great Fire of London. In 1667 the Treasury order system underwent a crisis of confidence when the Dutch raid on the Medway led to concerns about the likelihood of repayment. Dutch ships made their way up the Medway River and raided Chatham dockyard, capturing and taking home the ship *Royal Charles*. The Dutch were able to carry out this daring feat due to England's lack of money and resources, which meant that they kept the fleet in harbour and with only limited defences, and the belief that a peace treaty would soon be negotiated without further confrontation. A new supply act, voted through Parliament in February, was used to clear existing war debt, and there simply was not enough money to pay for supplies or the wages of sailors and dockyard workers, who had suffered delays in wage payments upon tickets for years and had resorted to stealing supplies in order to feed their families.[20] The non-payment of officers exposed the financial straits of the government and the shortfall of revenue to facilitate the war effort.

The credibility of government finance and fears of an invasion in London led to panic, and depositors descended on goldsmith bankers to withdraw their funds. One contemporary letter described how the Dutch raid caused 'such astonishment that every one went to his goldsmith to recall his moneys, but they were all sent back empty handed, and the King was forced to issue a declaration, to save the goldsmiths from persecution'.[21] The declaration made by Charles II that saved the goldsmiths also renewed confidence in the Treasury order system. Charles reaffirmed the ordered and sequential repayment of the money advanced to the government and secured upon the revenue, and further added that he would 'likewise hold firm and sacred in all future assignments and securities' so made, and 'will not upon any occasion whatsoever permit or suffer any alteration, anticipation or interruption' of that system.[22] This would prove to be a promise he would break less than five years later.

Despite peace with the Dutch in 1667, government finances did not improve. A report of 1668 from the Treasury revealed the dire straits of royal finances, with most revenue tied up in paying off prior debts, particularly the 'great anticipation under a devouring interest lying upon the Excise and Customs'.[23] Debts from the Second Anglo-Dutch War were joined by new military spending in 1670, which Charles committed to in the secret Treaty of Dover made with the French King Louis XIV. Under the terms of the treaty Charles would supply warships and infantry for a joint war against the Dutch and publicly profess Catholicism at an unspecified future date. In return Louis would provide a desperate Charles II with £160,000 up front, £1 million before the war, and £600,000 each year the war progressed.[24] While such payments would seem to improve Crown finances, a commitment to more military expenditure added to the financial problems already in motion due to long-term overspending.

In ten years from 1662 to 1672 public spending increased from £1.6 million to £2.5 million, of which approximately £1.2 million in 1672 was on military expenditure.[25] In October 1671, in an attempt to plug the deficit, the king and privy council met with some goldsmith bankers, 'in Lombard Street', to request a loan, but they refused.[26] Clearly, the bankers already had enough money tied up in public finances and were concerned for their reserves. Shortly after this meeting, the exact date is unclear, it was decided that a temporary stop on payments out of the Exchequer would take effect from the beginning of 1672. The formal announcement was not made until 2 January 1672, the date when the Stop was to take effect.

The Stop on the Exchequer

The Stop was not a blanket cease of all payments out of the Exchequer. It applied specifically to Treasury orders payable out of the ordinary revenue – the customs, excise, and hearth taxes – and fiduciary orders with no specific revenue stream attached. Taxes exempt from the Stop, and 'which are to be proceeded upon as if the Stop had never been made', were taxes levied by Act of Parliament to supply specific needs, and taxes levied 'upon the Fee-Farm Rents', or perpetual fixed rents paid on Crown lands.[27] The Stop also did not affect the payment of government departments and household or court officials.[28] Rather than a stop on payments, then, the events of 1672 have been described as a redirection of funds. Charles decided to utilise incoming revenue streams for military purposes, even though that revenue had been promised to pay off outstanding debts to government creditors. No money was stolen or requisitioned, but the Crown's actions had serious implications for the financial institutions underwriting government. The Stop was originally only to last for a year but was extended for another six months, before a further extension to January 1674.[29]

News of the Stop caused a run on goldsmith banks, as customers demanded the return of their funds. Without funds coming in, in the form of repayments of Treasury orders, affected bankers were unable to meet obligations to their clients, and they ran the risk of bankruptcy proceedings and debtors' prison as they stopped their own payments. The bankers were quick to act. Edward Backwell, Jeremiah Snow, and John Portman approached the king on 12 January to ask for interest payments and protection from arrests and debtors' prison, with which they had already been threatened by customers seeking their deposited funds.[30] Neither interest nor protection was granted. The goldsmith bankers had a poor reputation amongst politicians and government officials, who believed the goldsmiths' excessive interest rates on loans had debilitated the Crown and, as such, made little effort to help them.[31] The 1676 pamphlet *The Mystery of the New-Fashioned Goldsmiths* propagated the view that goldsmiths had taken excessive interest on loans, so much so that 'the King and Kingdom became Slaves to these Bankers'.[32] It has been suggested that the pamphlet was a 'government inspired attempt to justify the 1672 stop on the Exchequer', or at least a propaganda effort to smear the goldsmiths.[33]

Eleven of the 13 affected goldsmith bankers petitioned the King again in April 1673, once again requesting interest that had accrued since the Stop and for protection against lawsuits 'threatened' against them and their fears of 'being cast into gaoles'. They asked that £200,000 be set aside from a revenue stream to facilitate interest payments.[34] In May 1674 an agreement was made between the bankers and the Lord Treasurer for interest payments of 6% per year since the Stop, which amounted to £140,000, and which were paid in eight quarterly instalments from March 1675 to December 1676.[35] However, the bankers' customers had not received any repayment. In October 1675 a petition was presented to parliament by 'several and numerous Creditors of the Goldsmiths concerned in his Majesties Exchequer' in which they illuminated their financial struggles since the Stop, having 'not only failed of their Interest…but also of their Principal'.[36] This was to be solved in another agreement with the bankers.

Along with an agreement to pay interest, in 1674 the Lord Treasurer, Thomas Osborne the earl of Danby, ordered that a parliamentary committee investigate the full amount due to those affected by the Stop. The committee's report was published in 1676 and found that a total of £1,314,940 owed on Treasury orders was unpaid (Table 4.1). Of this, goldsmith bankers held £1,280,755 or 97.5% of the total debt. Danby proposed a repayment scheme whereby 6% interest on the bankers' debt, which with compounding interest in the intervening years had increased to £1,365,733, would be repaid annually from Christmas 1676. This amounted to a yearly sum of £81,944 to be divided amongst the affected bankers, paid from the king's hereditary revenue of excise. However, as the bankers had used the funds of their depositors, they were required to use their portion to repay their creditors, with each creditor receiving a yearly interest payment in proportion to the size of their deposit. The repayment fund was to be in perpetuity, so each creditor essentially received an annuity from the government on a long-term debt.[37]

To receive the annuity, the goldsmiths' creditors had to confirm with the Exchequer that they had deposited a principal sum at one of the affected goldsmith's banks and were therefore owed repayment. These transactions, between the Crown, the goldsmith bankers and their creditors, were recorded in a set of Assignment Books in the Exchequer of Receipt (The National Archives, E 406). Upon entering an assignment, the creditor was given an order that they could present annually for payment. These orders or annuities could be reassigned to heirs or a third party, also recorded in the Assignment Books, thus creating a form of long-term, transferable government debt. The interest payments were made regularly between 1677 and 1687 but stopped following the Glorious Revolution of 1688 when the Excise was again redirected to finance the Nine Years War (1688–1697).[39]

During this period of non-payment, surviving bankers conducted a lengthy legal suit against the Crown which would eventually achieve an Act of Parliament in 1701 that reinstated the repayment of debt.[40] The case was

Table 4.1 Amounts Owed to Goldsmith Bankers Following the Stop on the Exchequer[38]

Name	*Profession*	*Debt*	*Interest Due per Annum*	*Bankrupt/ Closed*
Sir Robert Vyner	Goldsmith banker	£416,724 13s 1d	£25,003 9s 4d	1684
Edward Backwell	Goldsmith banker	£295,994 16s 6d	£17,759 13s 8d	1682
Joseph Hornby	Goldsmith banker	£22,548 5s 6d	£1,352 17s 10d	1701
Gilbert Whitehall	Goldsmith banker	£248,866 3s 5d	£14,931 19s 4d	1685
George Snell	Goldsmith banker	£10,804 14s 5d	£653 13s 6d	
Bernard Turner	Goldsmith banker	£16,275 9s 8d	£976 10s 6d	
Jeremiah Snow	Goldsmith banker	£59,780 17s 2d	£3,586 17s	1690
John Lindsay	Goldsmith banker	£85,832 17s 2d	£5,149 17s 4d	1679
Robert Welstead	Goldsmith banker	£11,307 12s 1d	£678 9s	1695
Thomas Rowe	Goldsmith banker	£17,615 17s 8d	£1,056 19s	1683
John Portman	Goldsmith banker	£76,760 18s 2d	£4,605 13s	1678
Isaac Collier	Goldsmith banker	£1,784 6s 4d	£107 1s 1d	
John Thruston		£5,208 8s	£312 10s	
Isaac Legouch	Court jeweller	£5,870 3s 8d	£322 4s	
Robert Ryves	Goldsmith banker	£16,368 4s 4d	£982 1s 8d	1677
Edmond Turner		£4,592 11s 8d	£274 11s 8d	
Edward Chamberlain	Customs farmer	£706 1s 9d	£42 7s	
George Toriano	Merchant	£129 14s 8d	£7 15s 4d	
John Shaw	Merchant	£9,355 10s 4d	£561 6s 6d	
Francis Millington		£1,285 7s 2d	£77 2s 6d	
Henry Johnson	Shipbuilder	£1,388 11s	£83 5s 9d	
Robert Winne		£567 7s	£34	
Richard Lant		£1,844 0s 7d	£110 12s	
Isaac Alvarez	Court jeweller	£1,580 13s 4d	£94 16s	
William Gomeldon		£2,157 16s 5d	£129 10s	
Total		£1,315,338 1s 1d	£78,896 3s 2d	

entered into the Court of Exchequer in 1691 by Joseph Hornby and Sir Jeremiah Snow along with some assignees of other goldsmith bankers and taken out directly against the Crown. The first hurdle the bankers had to overcome was legal debate over the validity of the suit, which went against the protocol that the sovereign was immune from legislation. The suit was accepted by the courts in 1692, appealed to the Court of Exchequer Chamber in 1696 which found against the bankers and their creditors, but appealed again in the House of Lords by the bankers which decided in their favour in 1700 and ordered that interest payments be made from the Excise. However, six weeks later the Commons appropriated the Excise for the war effort (the War of the Spanish Succession). In 1701 it was ordered that repayments would begin in 1705.[41]

Under this agreement, repayment of interest declined from 6% to 3% and the debt could be redeemed by payment of half the principal amount.[42] From 1672 to 1706 the total amount of interest payments made was just £589,854.[43]

The aftermath

Historians disagree over the extent of the damage caused by the Stop. Some have argued that payments out of the Exchequer continued, that new goldsmith banks were established, and that there were very few bankruptcies immediately after.[44] Others have argued that the Stop caused a loss of confidence in the government, created an increased sense of risk in borrowing and lending, postponed the rise of joint-stock banking in England by a few decades, ruined the Crown's credit, and destroyed a generation of goldsmith bankers.[45] The longer-term impact and legacy of 1672 will be returned to in Chapter 6, but the remainder of this chapter lays out the more immediate effects.

One immediate result of the Stop was the removal from circulation of goldsmiths' promissory notes, which became unacceptable forms of payment. Those left holding such notes, which had no legal backing, had no recourse to assistance. The Treasury did not accept goldsmiths' notes again until 1680.[46] The rejection of goldsmiths' notes had a wider impact on the banking sector, both in practical terms and in terms of reputation. Practically it took away some key credit facilitators, and in terms of reputation it impacted goldsmiths' credibility and trust in the system. It also affected the inter-banker clearing system. Whilst other goldsmith bankers continued trading and clearing with one another, there was likely some loss of funds between bankers.[47] Treasury orders were also stopped but revived later. In limited application, using specific parliamentary taxes, and with appropriate safeguards the system had proved useful, and it was revived in 1677 for the 17 months' Assessment and known as the 'Exchequer Bill' from 1696.[48]

Aside from the bankers, there was a wider impact on credit in the capital. Horsefield estimated that about 2,500 depositors would have been affected and lost capital.[49] The Assignment Books record 2,349 entries between 1677 and 1705 of original depositors registering debt owed to them by goldsmith bankers.[50] The average debt owed was £475 and debts ranged from £36 to £12,942.[51] Some individuals losing out on this money would likely have defaulted on other financial obligations, thus extending the impact further to an unknowable amount of people.

The amount of money recouped by individuals in subsequent repayment plans is debateable. J. Keith Horsefield argued that over 34 years roughly half the debt in 1672, before any interest was added, had been repaid, thus giving an average rate of return of 1.5% per annum.[52] More recently Moshe Milevsky calculated a much lower rate. He argued that by taking into account the time value of money and assuming a compounding 6% interest over 34 years (making the initial debt grow to over £5 million), the return on the debt was 0.01% for an initial holder of the debt who continued to hold it until 1705.[53] However, Li further calculated that by utilising the secondary market for annuities, which was especially active during the period of regular repayment from 1677 to 1687, goldsmiths' customers could have recouped on average a third of their initial deposit.[54] The return is therefore dependent on how the debt is calculated and what data is used to trace the debt, but whichever way you look at it, bank customers experienced financial loss.

However, the market for credit was still alive and well and the events of 1672 did not affect all goldsmith bankers. The five goldsmith bankers who held 85% of the total debt (over £1.1 million) from the Stop – Vyner, Backwell, Whitehall, Lindsay, and Portman – were most negatively impacted, but the Stop affected those with lower amounts of debt too. Nine out of the 13 goldsmith bankers listed as Crown creditors were bankrupt before the end of the seventeenth century, and Hornby was bankrupt shortly after in 1701. The rate of survival and the nature of the surviving and newly established goldsmith banks after 1672 are the subject of the following chapter.

Notes

1 *At the Court at White Hall, January 2, 1671/2* (1672).
2 Bruce G. Carruthers, *City of Capital: Politics and Markets in the English Financial Revolution* (Princeton: Princeton University Press, 1996), p. 55.
3 C.D. Chandaman, *The English Public Revenue, 1660–1688* (Oxford: Oxford University Press, 1975), pp. 200–12.
4 Andrew Browning, *English Historical Documents, 1660–1714* (London: Routledge, 1996), numbers 100–102, pp. 265–72; Moshe Milevsky, *The Day the King Defaulted: Financial Lessons from the Stop of the Exchequer in 1672* (Cham: Palgrave, 2017), pp. 73–93.
5 R.D. Richards, *The Early History of Banking in England* (London: Routledge, 2012 reprint), p. 66.
6 Milevsky, *Day the King Defaulted*, p. 80.
7 Chandaman, *English Public Revenue*, pp. 285–7.
8 Robert Ashton, 'Revenue Farming under the Early Stuarts', *The Economic History Review* 8 (1956), pp. 311–2.
9 Christine Desan, *Making Money: Coin, Currency, and the Coming of Capitalism* (Oxford: Oxford University Press, 2014), p. 243.
10 Chandaman, *English Public Revenue*, p. 38.
11 Carruthers, *City of Capital*, p. 82.
12 George Downing, *A State of the Case, between Furnishing His Majesty with Money* (London, 1665).
13 Henry Roseveare, *The Financial Revolution 1660–1760* (London: Longman, 1991), p. 7.
14 Chandaman, *English Public Revenue*, pp. 295–6; Milevsky, *Day the King Defaulted*, p. 99; The Diary of Samuel Pepys, https://www.pepysdiary.com/, Monday 14 May 1666.
15 Downing, *State of the Case*, p. 3.

16 Carruthers, *City of Capital*, pp. 61–2; Desan, *Making Money*, p. 261; Chapter 2.
17 Henry Roseveare, 'Government Financial Policy and the Money Market in Late Seventeenth Century England', in Annalisa Guarducci (ed.) *Prodotto lordo e finanza pubblica* (Prato: Instituto Internazionale di Storia Economica, 1988), pp. 714, 731.
18 Henry Roseveare, 'Government Financial Policy and the Money Market in Late Seventeenth Century England', in *Prodotto lordo e finanza pubblica* (Prato: Instituto Internazionale di Storia Economica, 1988), p. 730.
19 J. Keith Horsefield, 'The "Stop of the Exchequer" Revisited', *The Economic History Review* 35 (1982), p. 511; Milevsky, *Day the King Defaulted*, pp. 118–20; Glenn O. Nichols, 'English Government Borrowing, 1660–1688', *Journal of British Studies* 10 (1971), pp. 98–9; Henry Roseveare, *The Treasury, 1660–1870* (London: George Allen & Unwin, 1973), pp. 31–3.
20 J.R. Jones, *The Anglo-Dutch Wars of the Seventeenth Century* (London: Routledge, 1996), pp. 174–7; Steven C.A. Pincus, *Protestantism and Patriotism: Ideologies and the Making of English Foreign Policy, 1650–1668* (Cambridge: Cambridge University Press, 1996), pp. 389–92; see also P.G. Rogers, *The Dutch in the Medway* (Oxford: Oxford University Press, 1970). For more on sailor's wage tickets and delays in payment, see Margaret R. Hunt, 'Frauds on Navy Pay and the Men and Women of Maritime London, c.1620–1740', *Past & Present* 265 (2024), pp. 108–38.
21 State Papers Online, SP 29/207 f.128, 'Jas. Thruston to Viscount Conway, Ragley'. 29 June 1667.
22 Milevsky, *Day the King Defaulted*, pp. 127–9; Browning, *Historical Documents*, Doc number 126, 'Proclamation Declaring the Inviolability of the Exchequer, 1667', pp. 341–2.
23 British Library Add. MSS 28,078, ff. 11–15, 'Scheme for settling his Majesty's expense upon the several Branches of his Majesty's Revenue, presented to his Majesty by the Lords Commissioners of his Treasury', 20 October 1668 – printed in Roseveare, *The Treasury*, pp. 120–4.
24 Milevsky, *Day the King Defaulted*, pp. 137–9; R. Hutton, 'The Making of the Secret Treaty of Dover, 1668–1670', *The Historical Journal* 29 (1986), pp. 297–318.
25 Carruthers, *City of Capital*, p. 54.
26 Browning, *English Historical Documents*, number 129, p. 344.
27 *At the Court at White Hall, January 2, 1671/2* (1672).
28 Horsefield, 'Stop on the Exchequer', p. 513.
29 *At the Court at Whitehall, January 2, 1671/2* (London, 1672); *At the Court at Whitehall, the Eleventh of December, 1672* (London, 1672).
30 William A. Shaw, *Calendar of Treasury Books*, vol 3, 'Minute Book: January 1672', 12 January 1672. Legal cases for example TNA, E 112/455/987, Executors of John White v Hornby, 1672.
31 Roseveare, 'Government Financial Policy', pp. 725, 729; Milevsky, *Day the King Defaulted*, p. 150.
32 *The Mystery of the New Fashioned Goldsmiths or Bankers. Their Rise, Growth, State, and Decay* (1676).
33 Ben Coates, *The Impact of the English Civil War on the Economy of London, 1642–50* (London: Routledge, 2016), p. 85.
34 SPO, SP 29/441 f.311, Petition of goldsmith bankers to the King, April 1673.
35 Shaw, *Calendar of Treasury Books*, vol 4, 'Minute Book: May 1674', 14 May 1674; Milevsky, *Day the King Defaulted*, p. 177.
36 SPO, SP 29/374 f.213, 'The creditors of the Goldsmiths concerned in the Exchequer to the House of Commons', October 1675.

37 Horsefield, 'Stop on the Exchequer', pp. 514–6; Ling-Fan Li, 'The Stop of the Exchequer and the Secondary Market for English Sovereign Debt, 1677–1705', *The Journal of Economic History* 79 (2019), pp. 176–200; *His Majesties gracious patent to the goldsmiths, for payment and satisfaction of their debt* (London, 1677).
38 William A. Shaw, *Calendar of Treasury Books*, volume 3, 1669–1672, p. xlviii; *History of Parliament Online*, https://www.historyofparliamentonline.org/.
39 Li, 'Stop of the Exchequer', pp. 181–6; Horsefield, 'Stop on the Exchequer', p. 518; *The deplorable condition of the assignees of sundry goldsmiths entitled by the letters-patents of King Charles the Second, to annual sums out of the hereditary revenue of excise* (London, 1697).
40 T.B. Howell, *A Complete Collection of State Trials and Proceedings for High Treason and Other Cromes and Misdemeanours*, volume XIV (London, 1812), pp.1–113.
41 Horsefield, 'Stop on the Exchequer', pp. 518–23; Desan, *Making Money*, pp. 281–7.
42 Li, 'Stop of the Exchequer', pp. 181, 185.
43 Milevsky, *Day the King Defaulted*, p. 181.
44 Richards, *Early History*, pp. 24–5; Shaw, *Calendar of Treasury Books*, Vol. 3, p. li.
45 Nichols, 'English Government Borrowing', p. 101; Stephen Quinn, 'The Glorious Revolution's Effect on English Private Finance: A Microhistory, 1680–1705', *The Journal of Economic History* 61 (2001), p. 595; Horsefield, 'Stop on the Exchequer', p. 528; Roseveare, *Financial Revolution*, pp. 22–3.
46 Horsefield, 'Stop on the Exchequer', p. 523, Milevsky, *Day the King Defaulted*, p. 172.
47 Stephen Quinn, 'Balances and Goldsmith-bankers: The Co-ordination and Control of Inter-banker Debt Clearing in Seventeenth-century London', in David Mitchell (ed.), *Goldsmiths, Silversmiths and Bankers: Innovation and the Transfer of Skill, 1550 to 1750* (London: Alan Sutton Publishing, 1995), p. 61.
48 Chandaman, *English Public Revenue*, p. 298; R.D. Richards, 'The Exchequer Bill in the History of English Government Finance', *Economic History* 11 (1936), pp. 196–7.
49 Horsefield, 'Stop on the Exchequer', p. 527.
50 Li, 'Stop of the Exchequer', p. 184.
51 Carruthers, *City of Capital*, p. 65.
52 Horsefield, 'Stop on the Exchequer', p. 523.
53 Milevsky, *Day the King Defaulted*, p. 189.
54 Li, 'Stop of the Exchequer', pp. 186, 185.

Bibliography

Primary sources

At the Court at White Hall, January 2, 1671/2 (1672).

At the Court at Whitehall, the Eleventh of December, 1672 (London, 1672).

British Library Add. MSS 28,078, ff. 11–15, 'Scheme for settling his Majesty's expense upon the several Branches of his Majesty's Revenue, presented to his Majesty by the Lords Commissioners of his Treasury', 20 October 1668 – printed in Henry Roseveare, *The Treasury, 1660–1870* (London: George Allen & Unwin, 1973), pp. 120–4.

The deplorable condition of the assignees of sundry goldsmiths entitled by the letters-patents of King Charles the Second, to annual sums out of the hereditary revenue of excise (London, 1697).

Downing, George, *A State of the Case, between Furnishing His Majesty with Money* (London, 1665).

His Majesties gracious patent to the goldsmiths, for payment and satisfaction of their debt (London, 1677).

The Mystery of the New Fashioned Goldsmiths or Bankers. Their Rise, Growth, State, and Decay (1676).

State Papers Online, SP 29/207 f.128, 'Jas. Thruston to Viscount Conway, Ragley'. 29 June 1667.

State Papers Online, SP 29/441 f.311, Petition of goldsmith bankers to the King, April 1673.

State Papers Online, SP 29/374 f.213, 'The creditors of the Goldsmiths concerned in the Exchequer to the House of Commons', October 1675.

TNA, E 112/455/987, Executors of John White v Hornby, 1672.

Books, edited collections, journal articles

Ashton, Robert, 'Revenue Farming under the Early Stuarts', *The Economic History Review* 8 (1956), pp. 310–22.

Browning, Andrew, *English Historical Documents, 1660–1714*, Part III 'Public Finance' (London: Routledge, 1996).

Carruthers, Bruce G., *City of Capital: Politics and Markets in the English Financial Revolution* (Princeton: Princeton University Press, 1996).

Chandaman, C.D., *The English Public Revenue, 1660–1688* (Oxford: Oxford University Press, 1975).

Coates, Ben, *The Impact of the English Civil War on the Economy of London, 1642–50* (London: Routledge, 2016).

Desan, Christine, *Making Money: Coin, Currency, and the Coming of Capitalism* (Oxford: Oxford University Press, 2014).

Horsefield, J. Keith, 'The "Stop of the Exchequer" Revisited', *The Economic History Review* 35 (1982), pp. 511–28.

Howell, T.B., *A Complete Collection of State Trials and Proceedings for High Treason and Other Cromes and Misdemeanours*, volume XIV (London, 1812).

Hunt, Margaret R., 'Frauds on Navy Pay and the Men and Women of Maritime London, c.1620–1740', *Past & Present* 265 (2024), pp. 108–38.

Hutton, R., 'The Making of the Secret Treaty of Dover, 1668–1670', *The Historical Journal* 29 (1986), pp. 297–318.

Jones, J.R. *The Anglo-Dutch Wars of the Seventeenth Century* (London: Routledge, 1996).

Li, Ling-Fan, 'The Stop of the Exchequer and the Secondary Market for English Sovereign Debt, 1677–1705', *The Journal of Economic History* 79 (2019), pp. 176–200.

Milevsky, Moshe, *The Day the King Defaulted: Financial Lessons from the Stop of the Exchequer in 1672* (Cham: Palgrave, 2017).

Nichols, Glenn O., 'English Government Borrowing, 1660–1688', *Journal of British Studies* 10 (1971), pp. 83–104.

Pincus, Steven C.A., *Protestantism and Patriotism: Ideologies and the Making of English Foreign Policy, 1650–1668* (Cambridge: Cambridge University Press, 1996).

Quinn, Stephen, 'Balances and Goldsmith-bankers: The Co-ordination and Control of Inter-banker Debt Clearing in Seventeenth-century London', in David Mitchell (ed.), *Goldsmiths, Silversmiths and Bankers: Innovation and the Transfer of Skill, 1550 to 1750* (London: Alan Sutton Publishing, 1995), pp. 53–76.

Quinn, Stephen, 'The Glorious Revolution's Effect on English Private Finance: A Micro-history, 1680–1705', *The Journal of Economic History* 61 (2001), pp. 593–615.

Richards, R.D., 'The Exchequer Bill in the History of English Government Finance', *Economic History* 11 (1936), pp. 193–211.

Richards, R.D., *The Early History of Banking in England* (London: Routledge, 2012 reprint).

Rogers, P.G., *The Dutch in the Medway* (Oxford: Oxford University Press, 1970).

Roseveare, Henry, *The Treasury, 1660–1870* (London: George Allen & Unwin, 1973).

Roseveare, Henry, 'Government Financial Policy and the Money Market in Late Seventeenth Century England', in Annalisa Guarducci (ed.) *Prodotto lordo e finanza pubblica* (Prato: Instituto Internazionale di Storia Economica, 1988), pp. 703–35.

Roseveare, Henry, *The Financial Revolution 1660–1760* (London: Longman, 1991).

Online databases

The Diary of Samuel Pepys, https://www.pepysdiary.com/

Shaw, William A., *Calendar of Treasury Books*, volumes 3–4: https://www.british-history.ac.uk/series/treasury-books-calendar

History of Parliament Online, https://www.historyofparliamentonline.org/

5 Later goldsmith bankers

The 1672 Stop on the Exchequer and its subsequent fall out did not signal an end to goldsmith banking. Some banks continued and others were newly established. However, from the 1690s onwards, a period identified as England's 'financial revolution', goldsmith bankers existed in a more financially diverse world. This chapter revisits Price and Melton's lists of bankers in 1677, 1687, and 1700 to examine the banks that survived 1672 and those that were established in the later seventeenth and early eighteenth centuries.[1] It looks at how goldsmith banking practices developed during the financial revolution and in competition with new institutions, most notably the founding of the Bank of England in 1694, which introduced public banking to Britain as opposed to the private banking carried on by goldsmiths.

In this chapter goldsmith banking is explored up until the 1730s. From the 1720s there was a declining association between goldsmiths and banking, and most goldsmith banks dropped any remaining links to the traditional goldsmith trade of making and retailing jewellery and plate.[2] From the 1730s onwards a greater number of surviving balance sheets and ledgers makes more detailed comparison between the banks' size and business trajectory possible. Many later goldsmith banks with surviving records have been written about.[3] However, these studies are mostly histories of individual institutions and are often not focussed on the history of the business itself but of the families and individuals behind it. This chapter provides a comparative, business-focussed exploration of the later goldsmith bankers.

Failures, survivors, and newcomers

In December 1682 the chronicler Narcissus Luttrell wrote that 'There are about 8 or ten of the considerable bankers or goldsmiths in London lately broke'.[4] Luttrell's statement demonstrates that the effects of the Stop on the Exchequer were slow to be felt and there were no immediate bankruptcies. Of the 13 goldsmith bankers directly caught up in the Stop, the first to go bankrupt, in 1677, was Robert Ryves, who was followed by two others by 1680. A further four went bankrupt in the early 1680s, and three in the 1690s and early 1700s.

DOI: 10.4324/9781003627449-5

Without limited liability, the entire estate of each goldsmith banker was legally at risk of being used to repay debts they owed to customers. Large-scale bankers like Sir Robert Vyner and Edward Backwell had numerous sources of funds to call upon to provide some repayment, including other sums held in government debt. For example, Vyner received arrears on a pension and for plate provided in his capacity as royal jeweller, as well as small amounts due on arrears for loans made against the hearth tax and for Navy expenditure.[5] Backwell was sent abroad on new missions as a royal agent, whilst also trying to distribute his estate,[6] which it was claimed had been largely 'mortgaged or sold', to demanding creditors as interest payments.[7] Through such methods they managed to keep some of their creditors at bay. Additionally, the agreements negotiated between goldsmith bankers and the state over potential repayment stalled other action against the bankers. However, the complexities of both Backwell and Vyner's bankruptcies ended in both posthumously being granted acts of parliament to settle their cases in the 1690s.

All those bankrupted by the Stop were City bankers. The West End bankers, who tended to have smaller businesses and were not involved in Crown lending, were not directly affected. It has even been suggested that West End bankers profited, as customers looked for other institutions to facilitate their financial needs. For example, as David Mitchell has argued, Thomas Fowle's business expanded post-1672, evident from recording in a pocketbook the 'product' of his lending from 1674 to 1692. In 1674 Fowle made just over £100 from moneylending. By 1677 this had risen to over £1,000, by 1689 over £3,000, and in the early 1690s over £6,000. His income from 1689 was enhanced by investment in new government debt issued to pay for the Nine Years War. Fowle also engaged in a greater volume of inter-banker clearing with fellow goldsmith bankers Blanchard and Child, suggesting an increase in account holders and transactions. Mitchell estimates, despite the absence of surviving ledgers or balance sheets, that Fowle's gross profit in the 1680s amounted to £4,000 per annum.[8] Despite business growth, Fowle's bank was much smaller than the City banks of the 1660s and early 1670s. In 1666 Backwell made £46,668 in interest receipts alone, mainly through his vast trade in government debt.[9]

Not all bankruptcies post-1672 were a result of the Stop. For example, in 1683 Benjamin Hinton failed and a commission of bankruptcy was taken out against him. Hinton's creditors were called to a meeting in July to subscribe to an agreement intended to settle his debts. The reason behind Hinton's bankruptcy is unclear. One of his creditors, London tradesman John Butcher, accused Hinton of inflating costs and of usury, charging 12% on some balances. Court cases across the 1670s and 1680s likely impacted Hinton's reputation and caused a run on his bank. Hinton's estate was sold in 1687 to satisfy customer repayments.[10] Similarly, John Hinde went bankrupt in 1685. The pamphlet published about Hinde's bankruptcy recalled that Hinde and his partner Kirwood had survived a run on their bank in the late 1670s, after which Hinde left the business. However, he returned in the early 1680s following the death of Kirwood, taking on a new partner, John Toplady, and investing in real estate. The pamphlet claims that certain creditors 'grew jealous', became suspicious of their activities, and caused a run on the bank. Hinde was arrested for debt and Toplady fled abroad to avoid prosecution. Hinde offered various compositions to his creditors but died in the Fleet Prison in 1686.[11] The examples of Hinton and Hinde demonstrate that even without involvement in state finance, goldsmith banking was a risky business, dependent on trust and reputation which could easily be undermined. Indeed, the survival rate of goldsmith banks in the later seventeenth century was low and few institutions survived long term (Table 5.1).[12]

Table 5.1 Goldsmith Bankers in the Later Seventeenth Century, Excluding Those Affected by the 1672 Stop[13]

Bank	*Location*	*First List Appearance*	*Bankrupt/ Closed*
John Addis	Lombard St	1677	1693
Atwell and Courtnay	Lombard St	1687	
John Bolitho and Mr Wilson	Lombard St	1677	1685
John Ballard	Lombard St	1677	
Child & Co	Fleet St	1670	
Job Bolton	Lombard St	1677	
Brassey and Caswall	Lombard St	1700	1758
Abraham Chambers	Fleet St	1687	
James Chambers	Fleet St	1687	
Mr Churchill	Strand	1677	
Coggs and Dann	Strand	1677	1710
Thomas Cook and Nicholas Cary	Lombard St	1677	
Cooke and Venables	Lombard St	1700	
Mr Cutbert	Cheapside	1677	
Charles Duncomb and Richard Kent	Lombard St	1677	
Bernard Eales	Lombard St	1687	
John East	Strand	1670	
John Ewing and Benj Norrington	Lombard St	1677	
Thomas Fowle, Fowle & Wotton	Fleet St	1670	
John Freame and Thomas Gould	Lombard St	1700	
Ralph Gerrard	Lombard St	1700	
Samuel Hankey	Fenchurch St	1687	
Henry Hankey	Fenchurch St	1700	
James Herriot	Fleet St	1677	
John Hinde and Thomas Kirwood	Lombard St	1670	1684
Benjamin Hinton	Lombard St	1670	1683
James Hoare/Richard Hoare	Fleet St	1670	
Roger and John Hudson	Fleet St	1700	
Jenkins and King	Lombard St	1700	
James Johnson	Cheapside	1677	1715
Mr Kenton	Fleet St	1677	
Mr Ketch	Strand	1677	

(Continued)

Table 5.1 (Continued)

Bank	*Location*	*First List Appearance*	*Bankrupt/ Closed*
Thomas Kilborne and Capill	Lombard St	1677	
Joseph Knight	Covent Garden	1687	
Henry Lamb	Lombard St	1677	d.1723
James Lapley	Cheapside	1677	
Richard Lassels	Strand	1687	
George Lewis	Strand	1700	
John Mawson and Comp	Fleet St	1670	
John Mead	Strand	1700	
George Merttins (later Michael?)	Lombard St	1700	1725
Middleton and Campbell	Strand	1700	
Edward Mompeson	Birchin lane	1700	
Richard Morson	Lombard St	1700	
Henry Nelthorpe	Lombard St	1677	
Thomas Pardo	Lombard St	1677	
Captain Pearce	Cheapside	1700	
Richard Peirson	Fleet St	1700	
Peter Percefull and Stephen Evans	Lombard St	1677	1712
William Pinckney	Fleet St	1670	
Phillip Pinckney	Temple Bar	1700	
Heneage Price	Strand	1687	1715
Thomas Price	Lombard St	1677	
Stephen Ram	Lombard St	1687	
John Rowland	Lombard St	1687	
Shales and Smithin	Lombard St	1687	
Michael Shrimpshaw	Fleet St	1677	1683
Richard Snagg	Lombard St	1687	1708
John Snell	Lombard St	1677	
Thomas Snow	Strand	1700	
Richard Stayley	Covent Garden	1677	1679
Humphrey Stocks	Lombard St	1670	
Robert Stokes	Lombard St	1700	
Andrew Stone	Lombard St	1700	
John Sweetaple	Lombard St	1670	1701
John Tassell	Lombard St	1670	
John Temple, John Seale	Lombard St	1677	1683
John Thursby	Lombard St	1677	
Benjamin Tudman	Lombard St	1700	
Bernard Turner and Samuel Tookie	Lombard St	1677	
Peter Wade	Lombard St	1677	
Wallis and Studley	Lombard St	1677	
Robert Ward, John Towneley	Lombard St	1677	
John Warner	Strand	1670	
Peter White and Churchill	Lombard St	1677	
Tho White	Lombard St	1677	
Joseph Wilson	Lombard St	1700	
Thomas Williams	Lombard St	1670	d.1697
William Wright	Covent Garden	1700	

One of the most successful survivors from the pre-1672 period was the bank of Blanchard and Child, which after Blanchard's death in 1681 became Child & Co. Child expanded the business to become 'one of the leading London banking houses' in the 1680s.[14] Child & Co was sold in the early twentieth century but the business continued, as part of various successor banking companies, under the Child & Co name in Fleet Street until 2022.[15] Another bank with longevity was Hoare's bank, opened in Cheapside in 1673 by Richard Hoare and moved to Fleet Street in 1690, where it still operates as a family bank today.[16] Backwell's legacy continued in the form of his apprentice Charles, later Sir Charles, Duncombe who started his own bank after he gained freedom from the Goldsmiths' Company in 1672. Duncombe's partnership with non-goldsmith Richard Kent lasted until Kent's retirement in 1688. Less is known of the nature and scale of Duncombe's banking activities after this date, although he appears to have still been active in 1694. Martin's bank later operated from the same premises but continuity between the two businesses is unclear.[17] Martin's bank began under Richard Smith in 1695, and Thomas Martin joined the firm initially as a clerk, becoming a partner from 1703. Martin's bank continued independently until it was bought by the Bank of Liverpool in 1918 and then absorbed by Barclays in 1968.[18]

Barclays bank traces its own origins to the goldsmith bank of John Freame and Thomas Gould, two quakers who went into partnership in 1690. The first Barclay to enter the bank was James Barclay in 1733, and the name of the partnership changed numerous times over the years as partners came and went. For ease the bank will be referred to as Barclays throughout. The bank retained a strong familial and quaker association into the nineteenth century, before expanding and merging with other banks to create a joint-stock bank in 1896.[19] The 1690s also saw the introduction of Scottish goldsmith bankers in London. The Scottish financial revolution was trailing behind its English equivalent at the turn of the eighteenth century, and Scottish financiers sought new opportunities in the English capital, most notably John Campbell, whose bank would later become Coutts, and later in the 1710s Andrew Drummond, both of whom had trained as goldsmiths in Edinburgh.[20] These banks will be looked at to varying degrees across this chapter.

The goldsmiths and the financial revolution

The 1690s financial revolution in England witnessed a dramatic increase in the type and number of financial institutions and instruments, and the introduction of public banking and the funded national debt. Historians argue that the groundwork for the financial revolution had been laid in the decades prior to the 1690s, including developments in private banking and in the organisation and practices of the Treasury.[21] The transformation in the relationship between Crown and government enacted by the Glorious Revolution of 1688 is also argued to have played a significant role in subsequent economic and commercial success, placing restrictions on the Crown's fiscal powers and encouraging greater trust in government securities.[22]

The financial revolution was largely driven by the government's need to finance ever more expensive wars. Wars with France following the accession of William III and Mary II in 1688 once again brought wartime financial issues to the fore. Increased taxation simply could not supply the finance required, despite the introduction of a new poll or land tax in the 1690s.[23] Warfare also impacted the already suffering coinage, which as a result of England's entrance into the Nine Years War in 1689 was clipped and exported as the exchange rate fell to facilitate the arbitrage between bills of exchange and bullion.[24] Alongside the usual request for private loans to bridge the state's funding gap, other methods of raising money were attempted, including lotteries, tontines, and annuities.[25] The most significant development in public finance, however, was the Bank of England which was formed in 1694. The bank was designed as a 'fund of perpetual interest', raising a sum of money that would be given to the state in return for yearly interest backed by tax revenue. The original sum raised was £1.2 million and was to be provided to the government in sealed bills and bank notes. Those committing money to the Bank of England held perpetual stock which could be traded as a liquid investment and provided 8% interest. From the outset the Bank of England was a note-issuing bank, providing bank notes payable to bearer as the goldsmiths had done.[26] The Bank, lotteries, annuities, and other schemes all combined to create the long-term funded national debt, turning Britain into what John Brewer described as a fiscal-military state, providing resources well beyond its income to enable it to triumph militarily.[27]

The Bank of England brought a significant change to the banking industry, ending the domination of the private sector. In the nineteenth century, historian Thomas Macaulay stated that 'All the goldsmiths and pawnbrokers set up a howl of rage' upon news of the Bank's formation.[28] Tension between the Bank of England and goldsmith bankers was clear at the outset. In a 1695 pamphlet Michael Godfrey, the Bank's first deputy governor, made comparisons between the Bank and goldsmith banks. He stated those depositing money at the Bank had the same 'Ease and security' of their money 'as if it were in the hands of the *Goldsmiths*'. Godfrey therefore acknowledged the goldsmiths' role in making the nation familiar with banking practices but was highly critical of the bankers themselves. He referred to money 'so *scandalously Clipt*' by the goldsmiths, money 'lost in *England* by the *Goldsmiths* and *Scriveners* Breaking', and the 'danger' posed by a handful of goldsmiths 'who were used to have *most of the running Cash of the Kingdom*'. In contrast the Bank of England was much safer and would reduce interest rates and expand the money in circulation. The Bank would only ever be 'injurious' to 'Banking Goldsmiths' who would be hindered from their 'Oppressive Extortion'. Godfrey suggested goldsmiths 'be limited to the selling plate and Jewels, which was their ancient and proper Trade'.[29]

The formation of the Bank of England has been characterised in the context of party politics which emerged in the later seventeenth century, viewed as a Whig creation that faced significant Tory resistance, with the Tories instead favouring a land bank based on agrarian rather than commercial wealth.[30] Gary DeKrey argues that a 'disproportionate share' of Tory leadership roles were filled with financiers, particularly goldsmith bankers. Fewer goldsmith bankers were involved in Whig politics, and those that were did not rise as high in the party as their Tory equivalents. He therefore argued that goldsmith banking was Tory-leaning.[31] Whilst some of the most successful goldsmith bankers did become Tory politicians, namely Sir Charles Duncombe, Sir Francis Child, and Sir Richard Hoare,[32] this was not true of all goldsmith bankers. For example, Thomas Martin was a Whig MP.[33] Additionally, Duncombe, Child, and Hoare were what Perry Gauci labelled the 'new leaders' of the banking sector, who like Backwell and Vyner before them were the most successful bankers of their day and obtained significant political roles, but should not be taken as representative of all goldsmith bankers at the time. As Gauci argued, whilst goldsmith bankers 'were quick to denounce the Bank, and fumed against its privileges', this may have been an immediate reaction to the business competition posed by the Bank, and not motivated by party political factionalism. In reality, and over time, goldsmith bankers, and bankers in general, were 'wary to avoid factionalism' and 'prepared to work with both parties in their longer-term interest'.[34] It would not have made good business sense for goldsmith bankers to exclude customers based on political allegiance.

Despite early tensions and fear of competition, there remained an important place for goldsmith banks in state and private finance. In terms of the state, the capital raised by the Bank of England, though extensive, still did not meet the costs of war, and goldsmith bankers remained key providers of loans to the government.[35] Goldsmiths also remained prominent as private bankers. Whilst the Bank of England did offer bank accounts, loans, and services to private individuals, it was primarily designed to supply the government.[36]

Private goldsmith banks offered a more intimate relationship with customers than the Bank of England. With the rise of the stock market and an increase in the number of securities available for investment, goldsmith bankers expanded their services in the management of clients' wealth.[37] Goldsmith bankers had long acted as agents for country landowners and the gentry, collecting rents and paying bills, but from the later seventeenth century they facilitated the buying and selling of stocks and shares, annuities, and lottery tickets on behalf of account holders.[38] Lotteries, both private and state-sponsored, grew in popularity in the 1690s, and goldsmiths often acted as receivers – selling the tickets, recording sales, and accounting to the manager.[39] As facilitators of other investments, most goldsmith bankers had by the 1690s stopped offering interest on deposit accounts. The attraction of a bank account was management services and 'convenience', enabling the customer to draw and collect money and direct payments, rather than accrue interest.[40]

This kind of activity was particularly prevalent amongst the West End banks, whose aristocratic and landed clientele had the money to engage in the stock market and required the services of a financial agent to facilitate it.[41] Bankers made profit acting as agents and brokers through fees and commission.[42] Hoare's bank was particularly engaged in this kind of work. Correspondence in the 1690s demonstrates the trust placed in bankers. In 1698 Lord Ashburnham requested Richard Hoare to dispose of his money in the Poll Tax or Coal Act, 'the performance of which I leave absolutely and entirely to you'.[43] Thomas Belasyse, Earl Fauconberg, opened an account with Hoare in 1692, which he used for 'bills to be Received of Merchants' and 'tradesmen', and from which to draw cash from. Belasyse also invested in numerous trading companies and stocks, which Hoare may also have facilitated.[44]

Acting as an agent was less prominent amongst the more mercantile City banks. For example, Barclays bank had significant mercantile connections, and Jacob Price identified a close association between Barclays bank and the eighteenth-century Chesapeake trade.[45] Both Freame and Gould were the sons of merchants and had interests in the Virginia trade, and James Barclay, partner from 1733, was the son of prominent linen merchant David Barclay, who conducted extensive exports to America. The partners were also stockholders in the Welsh Copper Company and the London Lead Company.[46] In the first balance sheet, from 1733, the entry under 'discount book', which recorded bills discounted and awaiting maturity, accounts for 66% of assets held by the bank.[47] In contrast, Hoare's bank had a loan register recording each loan made and the type of collateral offered up, from plate and jewellery to mortgages and stocks.[48] Barclays therefore fitted the mercantile City bank stereotype, primarily engaged in discounting bills of exchange and other bills for their mercantile customers rather than acting as a financial agent.[49]

New securities created in the financial revolution also provided new investment opportunities for goldsmith banks and other commercial institutions, which were liquid enough to facilitate cash-flow issues.[50] Using the records of Child's Bank, formerly Blanchard and Child, Stephen Quinn argued for a concurrent revolution in private as well as public finance, as 'Bankers and their customers began to use the improved financial instruments of the government to facilitate private lending'. He found that public debt was increasingly being used as collateral to secure private loans, and that goldsmith bankers increasingly invested in public debt. Child altered the composition of his business to take advantage of the greater availability of public debt and the high returns on it during war years. During peace time Child lowered his investment in public debt and instead supplied more private loans.[51] Hoare's bank saw a similar rise in the amount of loans backed by securities as collateral in the early eighteenth century. Prior to 1700, loans with plate or jewellery as collateral were most common, then from 1700 to 1710 this changed to mortgages, before securities took over as the favoured collateral in the 1710s with the rise of the South Sea Company.[52]

Whilst securities offered liquidity and potentially high profits, goldsmiths invested in public debt with caution. Child could have reduced his fractional reserve further to take advantage of high returns on government debt during the Nine Years War, but instead he maintained a reserve to liabilities ratio of between 40% and 60% to ensure that he could meet demand for withdrawals and even a potential run on the bank. This cautious approach, although based on the evidence of only one bank, suggests that the 1672 Stop loomed large in the mind of one goldsmith banker, and presumably many more; goldsmiths participated in government lending but ensured they were adequately protected from risk. The seeming 'reluctance of private bankers to decrease their reserve ratios' in the later seventeenth century appears to have continued, with Jacob Price suggesting that a 50% ratio of cash to liabilities was common for goldsmith banks in the eighteenth century.[53]

One exception amongst the post-1672 bankers was Sir Charles Duncombe, who invested significantly in government debt. Duncombe had extensive experience in government finance, partially learnt from his master Edward Backwell but also from his own experience as a revenue collector for the Hearth tax in 1670 and for the 18 months assessment in 1673. In 1674 Duncombe was joined in business by Richard Kent, an experienced financier who served as Receiver General of the Excise. Unfortunately, Duncombe and Kent's records do not survive but historians have used evidence from the Treasury Books to gain an insight into the amounts of money they lent to the government. From 1676 Duncombe and Kent lent directly to the Crown through the Exchequer, mostly to support the military and navy. They lent significant amounts, peaking in June 1681 when they were owed over £236,000. As G. E. Aylmer pointed out, this was substantially less than the amount owed to Vyner at the 1672 Stop but only slightly less than the amount owed to Backwell.[54] Without ledgers or balance sheets, there is no way to assess the bank's liabilities or how much of their customers' deposits were tied up in government lending, but Duncombe and Kent were clearly significant bankers.[55]

As well as dealing in new financial instruments, goldsmiths continued to circulate their own paper notes, although the volume issued declined across the eighteenth century as the Bank of England note issue increased. The Bank of England did not obtain a complete monopoly over bank note issue until later in the nineteenth century, and accepted goldsmiths' notes for subscriptions or payments, albeit under specific circumstances. First, the note had to be endorsed to the governor and company of the Bank of England. Second, the note was immediately sent out by a bank teller to be cashed at the shop of the goldsmith who issued the note, receiving metallic money from the goldsmith to honour the note. The Bank also set up a committee to deal with transactions between themselves and the goldsmiths, compile lists of goldsmiths who had refused or delayed payment, and draw up accounts of cash outstanding upon goldsmiths' notes. The goldsmiths in return dealt with Bank of England paper instruments, discounting bills and accepting notes.[56]

The financial revolution was not all plain sailing, and sometimes institutions failed. One of the most significant failures was the South Sea Bubble of 1720.[57] The South Sea Company was established in 1711, as a joint-stock company trading to South America with the intention of breaking the Spanish monopoly on trade in the region. The Company's capital of £10 million was raised not by subscription but by swapping existing government debt for company shares, which were more liquid for investors and reduced the revenue required for government to service its debt. The Company would receive 6% interest in perpetuity from the government on the debt. Some of the government debt exchanged for South Sea stock was the remaining debt owed to the goldsmith bankers after the 1672 Stop on the Exchequer. The intended trade was ultimately unsuccessful, but the Company continued to convert government debt into shares, and the share price rose beyond the value of the stock, creating a frenzy of speculation. Those who bought early and sold their shares before the bubble burst made record profits, but those who bought late lost money when the bubble burst and share prices plummeted.[58] Goldsmith bankers and their customers were amongst those invested in South Sea stock, and whilst some like Hoare's bank profited from its investment, others lost.[59] Like the 1672 Stop, the bubble created chaos in banking circles and caused some banks to collapse.[60] Unlike the 1672 Stop, the impact of the South Sea Bubble was more widespread and not concentrated in the hands of a group of goldsmith bankers.

The size and clientele of later goldsmith banks

As with earlier banks, there are few surviving balance sheets, ledgers, or other business records for later goldsmith banks, particularly in the early eighteenth century. Balance sheets, which record the assets (money owned by the bank, in cash or loans) and liabilities (money the bank owes to others, such as deposits) of a bank, are particularly useful as they provide a snapshot of how well the bank was performing at a specific time. Surviving records are patchy; some banks have surviving ledgers but no balance sheets and vice versa. It is therefore difficult to find a specific year to make comparisons between banks.

The earliest post-1672 balance sheets, which are the only surviving balance sheets for a goldsmith bank of this period as far as can be discovered, are from Child & Co in the 1680s. Limited comparison can be made between the assets – in private loans, government debt, and cash held in reserve – of Child & Co and of Duncombe and Kent in the 1680s. In 1681 Duncombe and Kent were owed £236,000 from the government and in 1684 £235,000.[61] In comparison, Child's balance sheet in 1690, a year after he began lending to the government on tally, shows assets of £161,383, of which only a percentage

Table 5.2 Number of Account Holders of Some Goldsmith Banks in the 1730s[64]

Bank	*Number of Customer Accounts*
Hoare's	917
Drummond's	305
Child & Co	237
Martin's	195*
Coutts	166
Barclays	84*
Total	1,904

would have been held in government debt.[62] Duncombe and Kent appears to have been a larger scale bank in the 1680s than Child & Co was in the 1690s.

A greater number of bank ledgers and balance sheets survive from 1730 onwards, and it is possible to gather data on the number of account holders and relative size of some of the banks. The total number of account holders at these banks is less than the total number of creditors recorded in the Exchequer assignment books for the earlier pre-1672 goldsmith banks (2,349). However, the Bank of England listed 1,585 customer accounts in 1730, significantly larger than any of the banks listed in the assignment books.[63] The number of customer accounts give some indication of the size of a handful of banks, mostly West End banks, but assets and liabilities calculated in balance sheets give a greater picture of the scale of the banks (Table 5.2).

1730s balance sheets survive for two City banks, Barclays and Martin's bank, and two West End banks, Child & Co and Hoare's bank. The exact dates of these balance sheets do not match up. For Barclays the earliest balance book is from 1733, for Martin's it is 1731, Child & Co has existing balance sheets in the 1730s for 1730 and 1735, and Hoare's balance books survive from 1719. Table 5.3 provides simplified versions of the balance sheets for three of the banks. Hoare's bank had assets in 1730 of just under £200,000, situating it somewhere between Child & Co and Martin's bank in terms of the size of its balance sheet.[65] Compared to the pre-1672 banks, the largest customer deposit balance from limited evidence in the Assignment Books was Vyner's bank, with £398,750, and Roseveare further estimated that Backwell had on average £420,000 deposited with him between 1664 and 1672.[66] None of the bank balance sheets in 1730 had liabilities close to these figures, but Child & Co exceeded those figures five years later with £464,297 in liabilities.[67] Roseveare's assertion that eighteenth-century banking houses did not match up to the scale of Restoration banks is therefore questionable, particularly by the mid-eighteenth century.[68] As in the earlier period, goldsmith banks varied in size and number of clientele.

The surviving balance sheets demonstrate the dominance amongst the later banks of Child & Co, which was twice as large as Martin's bank in the early 1730s. The pre-1672 dominance of large City banks therefore appears to have

Table 5.3 Balance Sheets from Barclays, Child's and Martin's Banks in the 1730s[69]

		Bank		
		Barclays 1733	*Child & Co 1730*	*Martin's Bank 1731*
Assets	Cash	£20,413 11s 1d	£143,325 3s 10d	£74,570 7s 9d
	Discounted bills	£49,293 4s 5d	£15 2s 6d	£83,177 4s 11d
	Overdrafts			£1,724 7s 3d
	Loans	£4,164 2s 9d	£173,876 11s 4d	
	Plate		£3,047 4s 10d	
	Total	£74,418 18s 3d	£320,264 2s 6d	£159,471 19s 11d
Liabilities	Customer deposits	£66,313 11s 4d	£299,900 10s 4d	£159,471 19s 11d
Cash to liabilities ratio		30.8%	47.8%	46.7%

reversed in the eighteenth century, with the West End banks, like Child & Co and Hoare's, expanding to provide significant private banking services. However, the evidence must be treated with caution. It only covers three (four including Hoare's) banks and is not representative of the entire banking sector. Additionally, the Barclays figures for the early 1730s were affected by changes to the partnership. In 1728 partner Thomas Gould died, removing his capital, and his son did not join the business in his place but set up his own bank which failed in 1731. In the mid-1730s James Barclay became a partner. Therefore, the years from 1730 to 1735 witnessed extensive disruptions, including lost partner capital and possible reputational damage due to the failure of the new Gould bank.[70] Barclays grew considerably by the end of the 1730s, with assets of £142,759 on the balance sheet in 1739, and in the 1750s reached a peak of over £300,000 in assets and liabilities which was not surpassed until the end of the century.[71]

Although the bank of Andrew Drummond has no surviving balance sheets before the late eighteenth century, the ledgers demonstrate its much smaller size relative to these other banks. Philip Winterbottom has shown that in 1730 Drummond's bank held a final balance in customer deposits of just £25,512. Some accounts had overdrafts, amounting to £15,259, so the overall net balance on accounts was £10,253 brought forward into the next year.[72] Drummond's bank was a much younger bank than the others in the 1730s. Drummond set up as a goldsmith in 1715, and his first bank ledger started in 1717.[73]

The balance sheets also allow insight into each bank's cash to liabilities ratio, or how much the bank held in cash compared to how much they had on the books in customer deposits. Table 5.3 reveals that had the banks experienced a run in the early 1730s Barclays could have met at least 30% of customer withdrawals with cash, and the others over 40%. Barclays lower ratio may have been a result of the lower amounts on the books in 1733. Later, from 1748 to 1754, Barclays kept a ratio of cash to liabilities of between 43% and 51%.[74] Cash to liabilities ratios afforded some protection from bank runs, covering typical demand for customer withdrawals and liquidity. However, as Stephen Quinn has argued, this could only carry bankers so far. Banks were always at risk from 'asymmetric information': even if the banker's personal forecast was positive and he was protected from shocks, the customer did not have the same level of insight. Customers relied on information publicly available to them. If there was rumour of government default, customers would be unaware of how stable their banker was and how much he held in government debt and could participate in a run to get their money back causing wider panic.[75]

Over the longer term, Temin and Voth gathered data on assets held by Hoare's bank, Barclays (listed as Freame and Gould), Martin's bank (listed as Duncombe and Kent), Child & Co, and Gosling's bank, a non-goldsmith private bank, from 1690 to 1750 to compare the relative size of the balance sheets of these banks. The evidence shows Child & Co significantly outstripped the others across the whole period, demonstrating significant growth in its extension of credit and the scale of the business. Child's bank grew from over £100,000 in assets in the 1690s to over £500,000 by 1750. Barclays was a consistently smaller bank than Child & Co, Hoare's, and Martin's across the eighteenth century.[76]

Exact figures for bank clientele in terms of status, gender, and location for each bank are hard to collect and would be an impossible task. However, it is fair to say that banking remained the preserve of the wealthy and was still largely London-centric into the eighteenth century. Generalisations about the occupational status of certain bank clients can be made. It was in the eighteenth century when the distinctions between West End and City banks solidified in terms of different clientele, with the West End banks attracting a greater number of landed and gentry clients than the more mercantile city banks. Additionally, some banks attracted clientele due to their own backgrounds or expertise. Barclays' customers were heavily influenced by the mercantile and Quaker backgrounds of its founders.[77] Hoare's bank customers, in contrast, were largely non-mercantile, landed aristocrats and professionals.[78] Drummond's bank largely served Scottish clients who had migrated to London after the 1707 Act of Union, and had a particularly strong military background, accounting for 16.7% of customers recorded in the ledger in 1730.[79] Coutts served the nobility and the Royal Family from early in its establishment, maintaining royal links to the present day.[80] Geographically, banking was still largely London-centric. However, from the 1750s banking extended out of the metropolis and new banks were set up in the provinces. Provincial banks often had links to London banks, who used them as correspondents, with the London bank holding balances and discounting bills for the provincial bank. This was before banks developed the practice of having branches in other locations.[81]

The decline of goldsmith banking?

England's economic landscape was transformed in the later seventeenth century. Far from becoming a bygone relic, goldsmith bankers kept up with and were integral to financial developments of the later seventeenth century. They co-existed with the Bank of England, learnt how to deal in new securities and stocks, and some developed banking houses that would have extreme longevity. However, the development of the financial sector meant that banking was becoming increasingly distinct from the trade of goldsmiths. Examining the growth of the banking sector in the long eighteenth century, Perry Gauci found that by mid-century a distinction had emerged between goldsmiths and bankers, based on their 'professional skills and requirements' as well as the scale of their businesses. Using samples of banking firms in 1677, 1736–40, and 1785–86, Gauci demonstrates a decline in the number of senior partners identified as members of the Goldsmiths' Company. In 1677, 80% were members, dropping to 50% by the 1730s, and 15% by 1785. The banking sector was increasingly made up of individuals from other trades and professions, sometimes comprising individuals with a shared religious alliance, and the sector also expanded outside the metropolis across England's provinces. The move away from goldsmithing went hand-in-hand with the increasing replacement or expansion of sole goldsmith bankers' businesses with a rise in banking partnerships, and new partners were selected for their capital, contacts, and specific expertise gained from different trade backgrounds.[82] From the mid-eighteenth century the terms banker and goldsmith were no longer interchangeable, and the banking industry developed as a distinct trade separate from any other industry.

Notes

1 F.G. Hilton Price, *A Handbook of London Bankers, with Some Account of Their Predecessors the Early Goldsmiths* (London: The Leadenhall Press, 1891); Frank T. Melton, *Sir Robert Clayton and the Origins of English Deposit Banking 1658–1685* (Cambridge: Cambridge University Press, 1986).

2 D.M. Joslin, 'London Private Bankers, 1720–1785', *The Economic History Review* 7 (1954), pp. 167–86.

3 Peter Temin and Hans Joachim-Voth, *Prometheus Shackled: Goldsmith Banks and England's Financial Revolution after 1700* (Oxford: Oxford University Press, 2013); Victoria Hutchings, *Messrs Hoare Bankers: A History of the Hoare Banking Dynasty* (London: Constable, 2005); R. Fulford, *Glyn's 1753–1953: Six Generations in Lombard Street* (London, 1953); G. Chandler, *Four Centuries of Banking as Illustrated by the Bankers, Customers and Staff Associated with the Constituent Banks of Martins Bank Limited* (London: Macmillan, 1964–68); H. Bolitho and D. Peel, *The Drummonds of Charing Cross* (London: George Allen and Unwin LTD, 1967); Edna Healey, *Coutts & Co 1692–1992: The Portrait of a Private Bank* (London: Hodder & Stoughton, 1992); M. Ackrill and L. Hannah, *Barclays: The Business of Banking, 1690–1996* (Cambridge: Cambridge University Press, 2001);

Peter Duncombe, *Great Goldsmith: The Life of Sir Charles Duncombe* (Chippendale: Leonard Communications and Marketing, 2001).

4 Narcissus Luttrell, A Brief Historical Relation of State Affairs, from September 1678 to April 1714, vol 1 (Oxford: Oxford University Press, 1969), p. 244.

5 Dorothy Clark, 'A Restoration Goldsmith Banking House: The Vine on Lombard Street', in *Essays in Modern History: In Honour of Wilbur Cortez Abbott* (Cambridge, Massachusetts: Harvard University Press, 1971), pp. 39–43.

6 Dorothy Clark, 'Edward Backwell as a Royal Agent', *The Economic History Review* 9 (1938), pp. 53–4.

7 *The Proposal of Edw. Backwell, Esq; to his creditors* (London, 1677).

8 David Mitchell, '"Mr. Fowle Pray Pay the Washwoman": The Trade of a London Goldsmith-Banker, 1660 1692', *Business and Economic History* 23 (1994), pp. 28, 32–6.

9 Henry Roseveare, 'Government Financial Policy and the Money Market in Late Seventeenth Century England', in Annalisa Guarducci (ed.) *Prodotto lordo e finanza pubblica* in *Prodotto lordo e finanza pubblica* (Prato: Instituto Internazionale di Storia Economica, 1988), p. 717.

10 Thomas Goodinge, *The Law against Bankrupts: Or, a Treatise wherein the Statutes against Bankrupts Are Explained by Several Cases, Resolutions, Judgments and Decrees, Both at Common Law and in Chancery* (London, 1695), pp. 267–75; *London Gazette*, 5 July 1683; *London Gazette*, 3 October 1687. Court cases for example: TNA, C 5/560/9, Stanley v Hinton, 1671; C 10/165/108, Turner v Hinton, 1672; C 7/520/18, Canham v Hinton, 1676; C 8/214/3, Butcher v Hinton, 1677; C 10/136/86, Shorte v Hinton, 1679; C 10/278/18, Butcher v Hinton, 1689.

11 *The Case of John Hinde Goldsmith with his Creditors justly stated Giving an Account to the World of the occasion of his Failing, his fair Proposals, and the Justness and Honesty of his Designs to all his Creditors* (London, 1685); *London Gazette*, 19 March 1687.

12 Gareth David Turner, 'English Banking in the Eighteenth Century: Bankers, Merchants and the creation of the English Financial System' (unpublished thesis), Durham University (2015), p. 32.

13 Melton, *Sir Robert Clayton*, pp. 236–42; Price, *Handbook of London Bankers*, 'Goldsmiths keeping Running Cashes' pp. 182–5; *London Gazette*, 'notices', https://www.thegazette.co.uk/all-notices?ref=topmenu.

14 Philip Winterbottom, 'Child, Sir Francis, the elder (1641/2–1713)', https://doi.org/10.1093/ref:odnb/5286.

15 https://www.natwestgroup.com/heritage/companies/child-and-co.html

16 Hutchings, *Messrs Hoare Bankers*.

17 Chandler, *Four Centuries of Banking*, pp. 94–103; R.D. Richards, *The Early History of Banking in England* (London: Routledge, 2012 reprint), p. 86; G.E. Aylmer, 'Duncombe, Sir Charles (bap.1648, d.1711)', https://doi.org/10.1093/ref:odnb/8236.

18 Ackrill and Hannah, *Barclays*, pp. 1, 55–7.

19 Ackrill and Hannah, *Barclays*, pp. 1–18, 40–1.

20 J.G. Checkland, *Scottish Banking: A History, 1695–1973* (Glasgow: Collins, 1975), pp. 9–16; Andrew McDiarmid, *Credit, Currency, and Capital: The Scottish Financial Revolution, 1690–1727* (London: Routledge, 2023), Chapter 6.

21 Roseveare, 'Government Financial Policy', pp. 708–9; Henry Roseveare, *The Treasury, 1660–1870* (London: George Unwin, 1973), pp. 17–45; Stephen Quinn, 'Tallies or Reserves? Sir Francis Child's Balance between Capital Reserves and Extending Credit to the Crown, 1685–1695', *Business and Economic History* 23 (1994), pp. 39, 41.

22 Famous argument made by Douglass C. North and Barry R. Weingast, 'Constitutions and Commitment: The Evolution of Institutions Governing Public Choice in Seventeenth-Century England', *The Journal of Economic History* 49 (1989), pp. 803–832. Questioned by other historians, for example: Anne L. Murphy, *The Origins of English Financial Markets: Investment and Speculation before the South Sea Bubble* (Cambridge: Cambridge University Press, 2009), p. 4; Christine Desan, *Making Money: Coin, Currency, and the Coming of Capitalism* (Oxford: Oxford University Press, 2014), pp. 288–95.

23 P.G.M. Dickson, *The Financial Revolution in England: A Study in the Development of Public Credit 1688–1756* (London: Macmillan, 1967), pp. 9–11, 46–7; Henry Roseveare, *The Financial Revolution 1660–1760* (London: Longman, 1991), pp. 33–4.

24 Stephen Quinn, 'Gold, Silver, and the Glorious Revolution: Arbitrage between Bills of Exchange and Bullion', *The Economic History Review* 49 (1996), pp. 473–90.

25 Roseveare, *Financial Revolution*, pp. 33–5; Dickson, *Financial Revolution*, pp. 41, 51–4; Anne L. Murphy, 'Lotteries in the 1690s: Investment or Gamble?', *Financial History Review* 12 (2005), pp. 227–46; Andrew McDiarmid, *The Tontine: A History* (Abingdon: Routledge, 2025), pp. 20–2.

26 Sir John Clapham, *The Bank of England A History*, vol. 1 1696–1797 (1944), pp. 14–21.

27 John Brewer, *The Sinews of Power: War, Money, and the English State, 1688–1783* (London: Unwin Hyman, 1989).

28 Thomas Babbington Macaulay, *Macaulay's History of England from the Accession of James II*, vol 4 (London: J.M. Dent & Sons LTD, 1953), p. 91.

29 Michael Godfrey, *A Short Account of the Bank of England* (London, 1695).

30 Steve Pincus, *1688 The First Modern Revolution* (New Haven: Yale University Press, 2009), pp. 366–9, 393–9.

31 Gary Stuart DeKrey, *A Fractured Society: The Politics of London in the First Age of Party 1688–1715* (Oxford: Clarendon Press, 1985), pp. 156–62.

32 Paula Watson and Perry Gauci, 'DUNCOMBE, Charles (1648–1711)', *HoP*, https://www.historyofparliamentonline.org/volume/1690–1715/member/duncombe-charles-1648–1711; Perry Gauci, 'HOARE, Sir Richard (1649–1719)', *HoP*, https://www.historyofparliamentonline.org/volume/1690–1715/member/hoare-sir-richard-1649–1719; Quinn, 'Tallies or Reserves?', p. 44.

33 R.S. Lea, 'MARTIN, Thomas (c.1679–1765)', *HoP*, https://www.historyofparliamentonline.org/volume/1715–1754/member/martin-thomas-1679–1765.

34 Perry Gauci, *The London Private Banker: A Social History, 1660–1825* (Oxford: Oxford University Press, 2025), pp. 138.

35 Perry Gauci, *The London Private Banker: A Social History, 1660–1825* (Oxford: Oxford University Press, 2025), pp. 141–2.

36 Joslin, 'London Private Bankers', p. 170.

37 Gauci, *London Private Banker*, pp. 82–6, 93–4.

38 Dickson, *Financial Revolution*, p. 76. Business conducted for account holders by power of attorney, see Joslin, 'London Private Bankers', p. 171.

39 David Mitchell, *The Wider Goldsmiths' Trade in Elizabethan and Stuart London* (London: Ad Ilissum, 2024), p. 329; Murphy 'Lotteries', pp. 227–46; Narcissus Luttrell, *A Brief Historical Relation of State Affairs, from September 1678 to April 1714*, vol 3 (Oxford: Oxford University Press, 1969), pp. 291, 318; Chandler, *Four Centuries of Banking*, p. 97.

40 George Selgin, 'Those Dishonest Goldsmiths', *Financial History Review* 19 (2012), p. 274; Jacob M. Price, *Capital and Credit in British Overseas Trade: The View from the Chesapeake, 1700–1776* (Cambridge: Harvard University Press, 1980), p. 81.

41 Joslin, 'London Private Bankers', pp. 176, 185.
42 Frank T. Melton, 'Deposit Banking in London, 1700–90', *Business History* 28 (1986), p. 49.
43 *Hoare's Bank A Record 1673–1932* (London: Private print, 1932), pp. 20–4, quote at 22.
44 British Library, MS 41255, Note-Book of Thomas Belasyse.
45 Price, *Capital and Credit*, pp. 71–2.
46 Ackrill and Hannah, *Barclays*, pp. 2–11, 15–6; P. G. M. Dickson, 'Barclay, David (1682–1769)', *Oxford Dictionary of National Biography*, https://doi.org/10.1093/ref:odnb/37149.
47 Barclays Group Archives, 131/71, 'Balance Sheet', Barclay, Bevan, Tritton and Co 1690–1888, 1733.
48 Temin and Voth, *Prometheus Shackled*, pp. 46–51.
49 Price, *Capital and Credit*, pp. 71–2, 90–1.
50 Dickson, *Financial Revolution*, p. 11.
51 Stephen Quinn, 'The Glorious Revolution's Effect on English Private Finance: A Microhistory, 1680–1705', *The Journal of Economic History* 61 (2001), pp. 593–615, quote at 613.
52 Temin and Voth, *Prometheus Shackled*, p. 50.
53 Quinn, 'Tallies or Reserves?', pp. 42–8, 40; Price, *Capital and Credit*, pp. 85–6.
54 See Chapter 4, Table 4.1.
55 Duncombe, *Great Goldsmith*, pp. 13, 46–108; Chandler, *Four Centuries of Banking*, p. 94; F.G. Hilton Price, *The Marygold by Temple Bar* (London: Bernard Quaritch, 1902), p. 69. For Duncombe and Kent's involvement with government finance and revenue, see William A. Shaw, *Calendar of Treasury Books*, volumes 3–8, accessible online: https://www.british-history.ac.uk/series/treasury-books-calendar
56 Joslin, 'London Private Banks', p. 170; Richards, *Early History of Banking*, pp. 154–5, 171–4.
57 Larry Neal, *I Am Not Master of Events: The Speculations of John Law and Lord Londonderry in the Mississippi and South Sea Bubbles* (New Haven: Yale University Press, 2012); Helen Paul, *The South Sea Bubble: an economic history of its origins and consequences* (London: Routledge, 2011).
58 Temin and Voth, *Prometheus Shackled*, pp. 26–8, 95–109; Dickson, *Financial Revolution*, pp. 90–156; Bruce Carruthers, *City of Capital: Politics and markets in the English financial revolution* (Princeton: Princeton University Press, 1996), p. 78.
59 Temin and Voth, *Prometheus Shackled*, pp. 110–9.
60 Turner, 'English Banking', pp. 68–72; Gauci, *London Private Banker*, pp. 17, 139; Chandler, *Four Centuries of Banking*, pp. 104–6; Joslin, 'London Private Banks', p. 171. Coutts Bank was badly affected as banker to John Law, the promoter behind the Mississippi Bubble in France: Healey, *Coutts & Co*, pp. 41–57.
61 Aylmer, 'Duncombe, Sir Charles', https://doi.org/10.1093/ref:odnb/8236.
62 Quinn, 'Tallies or Reserves?', p. 48.
63 Philip Winterbottom, 'Bank Clients and the Development of Personal Banking in London, 1672–1780' (unpublished thesis), Institute of Historical Research, University of London (2024), p. 87, fn. 104.
64 *London Gazette*, 'notices', p. 87 fn. 104; Chandler, *Four Centuries of Banking*, p. 117; Barclays group Archives, 131/71, 'Balance Sheet', Barclay, Bevan, Tritton and Co 1690–1888, 1733. *For Martin's and Barclays, the number of account holders comes from balance books rather than ledgers and reflects the number of customer accounts listed at the date of the balance sheet not the number for the whole year and may be incomplete.
65 Temin and Voth, *Prometheus Shackled*, p. 63.

66 For assignment books evidence, see Chapter 3; Henry Roseveare, *The Financial Revolution 1660–1760* (London: Longman, 1991), p. 19.
67 For 1735, see NatWest Group Archives, CH/206/2 f.128, Child & Co 'Casting up shop' ledger, 20 March 1735.
68 Roseveare, 'Government Financial Policy', p. 732.
69 Barclays Group Archives, 131/71, 'Balance Sheet', Barclay, Bevan, Tritton and Co 1690–1888, 1733; NatWest Group Archives, CH/206/2 f.123, Child & Co 'Casting up shop' ledger, 30 September 1730; Chandler, *Four Centuries of Banking*, pp. 117–8.
70 Ackrill and Hannah, *Barclays*, pp. 14–5.
71 Barclays Group Archives, 131/76, 'Balance Sheet', Barclay, Bevan, Tritton and Co 1690–1888, 1739; Turner, 'English Banking', p. 104.
72 Winterbottom, 'Bank Clients', pp. 156–7.
73 Bolitho and Peel, *The Drummonds*, pp. 17, 28–9.
74 Price, *Capital and Credit*, pp. 85–6.
75 Quinn, 'Tallies or Reserves?', p. 49.
76 Temin and Voth, *Prometheus Shackled*, pp. 63, 144.
77 Ackrill and Hannah, *Barclays*, pp. 8, 32.
78 Anne Laurence, 'The Emergence of a Private Clientele for Banks in the Early Eighteenth Century: Hoare's Bank and Some Women Customers', *The Economic History Review* 61 (2008), p. 565.
79 McDiarmid, *Credit, Currency, and Capital*, Chapter 6; Winterbottom, 'Bank Clients', p. 92; Melton, 'Deposit Banking', pp. 44–5.
80 Healey, *Coutts & Co*, pp. 6, 17, 30, 33, 90–1.
81 L.S. Presnell, *Country Banking in the Industrial Revolution* (Oxford: Clarendon Press, 1956), pp. 75–84; Iain Black, 'Private Banking in London's West End, 1750–1830', *The London Journal* 28 (2003), p. 31.
82 Gauci, *London Private Banker*, pp. 20, 14, 18–9, 24–34.

Bibliography

Primary sources

Barclays Group Archives, 131/71, 'Balance Sheet', Barclay, Bevan, Tritton and Co 1690–1888, 1733.

Barclays Group Archives, 131/76, 'Balance Sheet', Barclay, Bevan, Tritton and Co 1690–1888, 1739.

British Library, MS 41255, Note-Book of Thomas Belasyse.

The Case of John Hinde Goldsmith with his Creditors justly stated Giving an Account to the World of the occasion of his Failing, his fair Proposals, and the Justness and Honesty of his Designs to all his Creditors (London, 1685).

Godfrey, Michael, *A Short Account of the Bank of England* (London, 1695).

Goodinge, Thomas, *The Law against Bankrupts: Or, A Treatise Wherein the Statutes against Bankrupts Are Explained by Several Cases, Resolutions, Judgments and Decrees, Both at Common Law and in Chancery* (London, 1695).

Luttrell, Narcissus, *A Brief Historical Relation of State Affairs, from September 1678 to April 1714*, vol 1 (Oxford: Oxford University Press, 1969).

Luttrell, Narcissus, *A Brief Historical Relation of State Affairs, from September 1678 to April 1714*, vol 3 (Oxford: Oxford University Press, 1969).

NatWest Group Archives, CH/206/2 f.123, Child & Co 'Casting up shop' ledger, 30 September 1730.

NatWest Group Archives, CH/206/2 f.128, Child & Co 'Casting up shop' ledger, 20 March 1735.
The Proposal of Edw. Backwell, Esq; to his creditors (London, 1677).
TNA, C 5/560/9, Stanley v Hinton, 1671.
TNA, C 10/165/108, Turner v Hinton, 1672.
TNA, C 7/520/18, Canham v Hinton, 1676.
TNA, C 8/214/3, Butcher v Hinton, 1677.
TNA, C 10/136/86, Shorte v Hinton, 1679.
TNA, C 10/278/18, Butcher v Hinton, 1689.

Books, edited collections, and journal articles

Ackrill, M., and L. Hannah, *Barclays: The Business of Banking, 1690–1996* (Cambridge: Cambridge University Press, 2001).
Black, Iain S., 'Private Banking in London's West End, 1750–1830', *The London Journal* 28 (2003), pp. 29–59.
Brewer, John, *The Sinews of Power: War, Money, and the English State, 1688–1783* (London: Unwin Hyman, 1989).
Bolitho, H., and D. Peel, *The Drummonds of Charing Cross* (London: George Allen & Unwin LTD, 1967).
Carruthers, Bruce G., *City of Capital: Politics and Markets in the English Financial Revolution* (Princeton: Princeton University Press, 1996).
Chandler, G., *Four Centuries of Banking as Illustrated by the Bankers, Customers and Staff Associated with the Constituent Banks of Martins Bank Limited* (London: B.T. Batsford LMT, 1964–68).
Checkland, J.G., *Scottish Banking: A History, 1695–1973* (Glasgow: Collins, 1975).
Clapham, Sir John, *The Bank of England A History*, vol. 1 1696–1797 (Cambridge: Cambridge University Press,1945).
Clark, Dorothy, 'Edward Backwell as a Royal Agent', *The Economic History Review* 9 (1938), pp. 45–55.
Clark, Dorothy, 'A Restoration Goldsmith-Banking House: The Vine on Lombard Street', in *Essays in Modern English History: In Honour of Wilbur Cortez Abbott* (Cambridge, Massachusetts: Harvard University Press, 1971), Cambridge, Massachusetts: Harvard University Press, pp. 3–47.
DeKrey, Gary Stuart, *A Fractured Society: The Politics of London in the First Age of Party 1688–1715* (Oxford: Clarendon Press, 1985).
Desan, Christine, *Making Money: Coin, Currency, and the Coming of Capitalism* (Oxford: Oxford University Press, 2014).
Dickson, P.G.M., *The Financial Revolution in England: A Study in the Development of Public Credit 1688–1756* (London: Macmillan, 1967).
Duncombe, Peter, *Great Goldsmith: The Life of Sir Charles Duncombe* (Chippendale: Leonard Communications and Marketing, 2001).
Fulford, R., *Glyn's 1753–1953: Six Generations in Lombard Street* (London: Macmillan, 1953).
Gauci, Perry, *The London Private Banker: A Social History, 1660–1825* (Oxford: Oxford University Press, 2025).
Healey, Edna, *Coutts & Co 1692–1992: The Portrait of a Private Bank* (London: Hodder & Stoughton, 1992).

Hoare's Bank a Record 1673–1932 (London: Private print, 1932).
Horsefield, J. Keith, *British Monetary Experiments 1650–1710* (London: G. Bell and Sons, 1960).
Hutchings, Victoria, *Messrs Hoare Bankers: A History of the Hoare Banking Dynasty* (London: Constable, 2005).
Joslin, D.M., 'London Private Bankers, 1720–1785', *The Economic History Review* 7 (1954), pp. 167–86.
Laurence, Anne, 'The Emergence of a Private Clientele for Banks in the Early Eighteenth Century: Hoare's Bank and Some Women Customers', *The Economic History Review* 61 (2008), pp. 565–86.
Macaulay, Thomas Babbington, *Macaulay's History of England from the Accession of James II*, vol 4 (London: J.M. Dent & Sons LTD, 1953).
McDiarmid, Andrew, *Credit, Currency, and Capital: The Scottish Financial Revolution, 1690–1727* (London: Routledge, 2023).
McDiarmid, Andrew, *The Tontine: A History* (Abingdon: Routledge, 2025).
Melton, Frank T., *Sir Robert Clayton and the Origins of English Deposit Banking 1658–1685* (Cambridge: Cambridge University Press, 1986).
Melton, Frank T., 'Deposit Banking in London, 1700–90', *Business History* 28 (1986), pp. 40–50.
Mitchell, David, '"Mr. Fowle Pray Pay the Washwoman": The Trade of a London Goldsmith-Banker, 1660 1692', *Business and Economic History* 23 (1994), pp. 27–38.
Mitchell, David, *The Wider Goldsmiths' Trade in Elizabethan and Stuart* London (Ad Ilissum, London, 2024).
Murphy, Anne L., 'Lotteries in the 1690s: Investment or Gamble?', *Financial History Review* 12 (2005), pp. 227–46.
Neal, Larry, *I Am Not Master of Events: The Speculations of John Law and Lord Londonderry in the Mississippi and South Sea Bubbles* (New Haven: Yale University Press, 2012).
North Douglass, C., and Barry R. Weingast, 'Constitutions and Commitment: The Evolution of Institutions Governing Public Choice in Seventeenth-Century England', *The Journal of Economic History* 49 (1989), pp. 803–32.
Paul, Helen, *The South Sea Bubble: An Economic History of Its Origins and Consequences* (London: Routledge, 2011).
Pincus, Steve, *1688 The First Modern Revolution* (New Haven: Yale University Press, 2009).
Presnell, L.S., *Country Banking in the Industrial Revolution* (Oxford: Clarendon Press, 1956).
Price, F.G. Hilton, *A Handbook of London Bankers, with Some Account of Their Predecessors the Early Goldsmiths* (London: The Leadenhall Press, 1891).
Price, F.G. Hilton, *The Marygold by Temple Bar* (London: Bernard Quaritch, 1902).
Price, Jacob M., *Capital and Credit in British Overseas Trade: The View from the Chesapeake, 1700–1776* (Cambridge: Harvard University Press, 1980).
Quinn, Stephen, 'Tallies or Reserves? Sir Francis Child's Balance between Capital Reserves and Extending Credit to the Crown, 1685–1695', *Business and Economic History* 23 (1994), pp. 39–51.
Quinn, Stephen, 'Gold, Silver, and the Glorious Revolution: Arbitrage between Bills of Exchange and Bullion', *The Economic History Review* 49 (1996), pp. 473–90.

Quinn, Stephen, 'The Glorious Revolution's Effect on English Private Finance: A Microhistory, 1680–1705', *The Journal of Economic History* 61 (2001), pp. 593–615.

Richards, R.D., *The Early History of Banking in England* (London: Routledge, 2012 reprint).

Roseveare, Henry, *The Treasury, 1660–1870* (London: George Unwin, 1973).

Roseveare, Henry, 'Government Financial Policy and the Money Market in Late Seventeenth Century England', in Annalisa Guarducci (ed.) *Prodotto lordo e finanza pubblica* (Prato: Instituto Internazionale di Storia Economica, 1988), edited by Annalisa Guarducci, pp. 703–35.

Roseveare, Henry, *The Financial Revolution 1660–1760* (London: Longman, 1991).

Selgin, George, 'Those Dishonest Goldsmiths', *Financial History Review* 19 (2012), pp. 269–88.

Temin, Peter, and Hans Joachim-Voth, *Prometheus Shackled: Goldsmith Banks and England's Financial Revolution after 1700* (Oxford: Oxford University Press, 2013).

Turner, Gareth David, 'English Banking in the Eighteenth Century: Bankers, Merchants and the creation of the English Financial System' (unpublished thesis), Durham University (2015).

Winterbottom, Philip, 'Bank Clients and the Development of Personal Banking in London, 1672–1780' (unpublished thesis), Institute of Historical Research, University of London (2024).

Online databases

London Gazette, https://www.thegazette.co.uk/all-notices?ref=topmenu

Oxford Dictionary of National Biography, https://www.oxforddnb.com/

Shaw, William A. *Calendar of Treasury Books*, volumes 3–8: https://www.british-history.ac.uk/series/treasury-books-calendar

6 The legacy of goldsmith banking

In the 1940s historian John Clapham stated that 'The dependence of Charles II's government on them [the goldsmith bankers] – especially on Backwell and Vyner – is known to every schoolboy'.[1] Regardless of how true this was at the time, it is certainly not true today. Whilst some goldsmith banks still survive today, the links between goldsmiths and banking are largely forgotten in modern Britain. The foundation of the Bank of England is common knowledge, but much less is generally known about what came before, and the financial history of England is absent from the school curriculum. In academic circles, the emphasis on the financial revolution in economic history has focussed attention on the 1690s onwards, and goldsmiths appear in these narratives as minor figures alongside the Bank of England and the variety of new financial institutions taking shape.

Lack of knowledge or recognition of the goldsmiths' place in financial history could be because there are few surviving banks that can trace their origins back to the seventeenth century. Only Barclays, Coutts, and Hoare & Co can now make this claim. Of these three, Hoare's bank is the oldest and the only private bank, which remains under the management of descendants of the original goldsmith Richard Hoare. Child & Co could be added to this list and would trump Hoare's as the oldest surviving bank started in the 1660s, but it no longer existed as a bank in its own name after 2022. Another bank no longer extant claimed even greater longevity. Martin's bank, which was absorbed by Barclays in the 1960s, claimed an origin dating back to 1563, Elizabethan goldsmiths, and royal financial agent Sir Thomas Gresham. However, the claim for longevity centred not on the business but on the bank's premises, the Grasshopper in Lombard Street. Despite the premises and sign remaining the same, there was no continuous business link between the numerous banking firms located at the Grasshopper.[2] Banks with links to seventeenth-century goldsmiths utilise their history and longevity as part of their marketing strategy, emphasising their historic roots in the banking sector and ability to weather a variety of financial storms over the course of 300-plus years.

Over time the identity of a bank and of bank partners has declined in importance. Banking in the seventeenth century was a highly personal affair;

DOI: 10.4324/9781003627449-6

it relied on the reputation and credit of both banker and customer. Banking was also reserved for the wealthy few, so personalised service was the norm amongst an elite banking community. Nowadays banks are used by everyone, operate as limited companies, and, apart from Hoare & Co, are faceless entities. Whilst individuals still need to trust a bank, that trust does not derive from the personal attributes of a banker. The personal, and historic, attributes of a bank are not sought after qualities in an increasingly digital and impersonal world.

Goldsmiths' contribution to banking in England

Goldsmith bankers were undoubtedly the founders of the British banking sector. Whilst scrivener banks were probably the first to accept deposits and function as financial agents, it was under the goldsmiths that these practices expanded into fractional reserve businesses, and goldsmith bankers built clearing networks amongst themselves to facilitate the circulation of financial instruments. Goldsmiths familiarised a generation with banking practices; facilitated the expansion of trade through issuing, accepting, and discounting bills of exchange; and, prior to and after the formation of the Bank of England, acted as major lenders to Crown and government. One of the most important functions of the goldsmith bankers, as Stephen Quinn has argued, was as intermediaries, providing liquid investments to customers and pooling them to invest in the more illiquid instruments of government debt and other large assets.[3]

One major contribution of goldsmith bankers to English finance was their popularisation of the promissory note payable to the bearer, defined by many historians as 'the forerunners of bankers' notes and paper currency'.[4] More recently, historians have stressed the differences between goldsmiths' promissory notes and paper money, emphasising the limited circulation of goldsmiths' notes and the lack of direct correspondence between the notes and the amount of physical coin held by the banker. Goldsmiths' notes were both instruments of credit and promises to pay. They were not universally recognised and could be refused as payment. However, the notes certainly came close to functioning as money within the London area and made the public familiar with bank notes and cheques, which was fundamental to the later success of paper money.[5]

There are obviously some caveats to the goldsmiths' success. Goldsmith bankers had limited exposure beyond a largely London-centric wealthy elite, who made up most of their customers. The spread of banking practices and familiarity with them outside of the capital and amongst the lower social orders was therefore a much longer process. The number of banks in London rapidly increased in the second half of the eighteenth century, providing services for a greater proportion of the population.[6] This was matched by the founding of banks in England's provinces in the later eighteenth century, which 'established the bank as a familiar sight in high streets across the country'.[7]

The failure of many goldsmith banks also questions their impact. The survival rate of banks in the later seventeenth and early eighteenth centuries shows a high turnover of businesses and limited longevity.[8] However, failure is expected in nascent industries. From the 1660s to the 1730s bankers were impacted by fire, numerous wars, the Stop on the Exchequer, the growth of the stocks market, the formation of the Bank of England, and the South Sea Bubble. This is in addition to disputes between creditors and bankers over financial practices, and instances of fraud.[9] Whilst some banks weathered the financial storms, others did not. But insolvency and bankruptcy did not affect the entire sector, and new banks were established as others collapsed.

Goldsmith bankers were central figures in the 1672 Stop on the Exchequer, which had significant implications for England's financial development. In the short term, the Stop hindered credit networks and caused insolvency. However, in the long term the solution to the Stop, the annuities given to the goldsmiths' creditors, unwittingly established the early basis of what would become the national debt. The annuities, unlike the Treasury Orders, inspired a reasonably active secondary market and were used for endowments, dowries, and as security for debt settlements and loans.[10] Christine Desan even posited the Treasury order in a more positive light, arguing that the development of Treasury orders, which raised funds for the Crown but also offered monetary incentives to individuals via interest payments and assignability, 'set England on its path towards the modern political economy by offering people a way to profit while furthering the public fisc'.[11] As mediators between the public and the government, discounting orders and providing more liquid investments, the goldsmiths were key to this development.

Desan further argued that the resolution of the case of the bankers in 1700, their efforts to receive repayment of the debt owed from 1672, 'changed the design of public debt'. She argued that the outcome of this case was more important than the constitutional changes wrought by the 1688 Glorious Revolution, which Douglass North and Barry Weingast famously argued was vital to the development of public finance and the national debt. Prior to 1688 the Crown held considerable fiscal power, deciding how and on what money was spent. Following the revolution, fiscal power was largely transferred to Parliament, which gained the ability to oversee how public funds were spent and place constraints on the Crown. The new system prevented arbitrary seizure or redirection of funds, was backed up by a 'politically independent judiciary', and inspired 'credible commitment', or confidence that the government would honour its financial obligations.[12] However, Desan argues that constitutional change alone was not enough. Legal recognition of the altered state of public finance was required. This came in the form of the goldsmith bankers' legal case over the 1672 debt, which the bankers won. Their success demonstrated that public debt would henceforth be protected by law in the same way as private debt: the unique position of the monarch was disabled and any obligations made under bond and contract were to be treated the same as for any other individual.[13] Whilst the government would continue to default on debts in the future, legal precedent was set by this case, and mechanisms put in place for recovery. Similarly, Stephen Quinn has also placed the goldsmiths in a more important light regarding the development of public debt. He argued that as well as constitutional change, expanding government debt 'also required a banking system to connect savers and the English Treasury'. Such a banking system was created by the goldsmith bankers, laying the foundations for Britain to become a dominant world power in the eighteenth century.[14]

Conclusion

Goldsmith banks and bankers were crucial to the development of the British banking sector. Over the course of a century, they transformed from makers and retailers of plate and jewellery, into pawnbrokers and moneylenders, and finally into fully fledged banking businesses, shaking off any final remaining links to the goldsmiths' craft in the first half of the eighteenth century. The practices they instituted, particularly fractional reserve, created a banking system that was unique in Europe at the time and allowed for significant economic, mercantile, industrial, and military growth.

The story of goldsmith banking is hampered by limited source material. Surviving business records are a rarity. Other records, particularly government and legal records, can provide another, less systematic and more qualitative, way to analyse goldsmith banking. Whilst the larger longer-living banks have taken centre stage, further research could uncover more details about the sector by investigating the practices and interactions of smaller and lesser-known goldsmith bankers. There could even be some business records hidden away in an archive yet to be studied. Further research into goldsmith banking would expand our knowledge of this important sector, the customers it served, and its wider impact on finance and commerce.

Notes

1 Sir John Clapham, *The Bank of England A History*, vol. 1 1696–1797 (Cambridge: Cambridge University Press,1945), p. 11.
2 R.D. Richards, *The Early History of Banking in England* (London: Routledge, 2012 reprint), pp. 8, 88, 229.
3 Stephen Quinn, 'Banking before the Bank: London's Unregulated Goldsmith-bankers, 1660–1694' (unpublished thesis), University of Illinois (1994), pp. 2–18.
4 Frank T. Melton, 'Goldsmith Notes, 1654–1655', *Journal of the Society of Archivists* 6 (April 1978), p. 30; Richards, *The Early History*, p. 40.
5 Christine Desan, *Making Money: Coin, Currency, and the Coming of Capitalism* (Oxford: Oxford University Press, 2014), pp. 262, 300; Stephen Quinn, 'Goldsmith-Banking: Mutual Acceptance and Interbank Clearing in Restoration London', *Explorations in Economic History* 34 (1997), p. 427.

6 Gareth David Turner, 'English Banking in the Eighteenth Century: Bankers, Merchants and the Creation of the English Financial System' (unpublished thesis), Durham University (2015), p. 68.
7 Perry Gauci, *The London Private Banker: A Social History, 1660–1825* (Oxford: Oxford University Press, 2025), p. 7; L.S. Presnell, *Country Banking in the Industrial Revolution* (Oxford: Clarendon Press, 1956), pp. 2, 4–8.
8 Chapter 5; D.M. Joslin, 'London Private Bankers, 1720–1785', *The Economic History Review* 7 (1954), p. 174.
9 For example, Hinde and Hinton, Chapter 5 p. For bankruptcy because of fraud, see the bankruptcy of John Coggs and John Dann, who bankrolled Thomas Brerewood in the notorious Pitkin Affair, in which Brerewood and his partner Thomas Pitkin conducted a 'bust out' fraud on numerous creditors, in Emily Kadens, 'The Pitkin Affair: A Study of Fraud in Early English Bankruptcy', *American Bankruptcy Law Journal* 84 (2010), pp. 543–64.
10 Henry Roseveare, *The Financial Revolution 1660–1760* (London: Longman, 1991), p. 22; Henry Roseveare, 'Prejudice and Policy: Sir George Downing as Parliamentary Entrepreneur', in D.C. Coleman and Peter Mathias (eds.), *Enterprise and History: Essays in Honour of Charles Wilson* (Cambridge: Cambridge University Press, 1984), p. 146; Ling-Fan Li, 'The Stop of the Exchequer and the Secondary Market for English Sovereign Debt, 1677–1705', *The Journal of Economic History* 79 (2019), p. 188.
11 Desan, *Making Money*, pp. 279–80.
12 Douglass C. North and Barry R. Weingast, 'Constitutions and Commitment: The Evolution of Institutions Governing Public Choice in Seventeenth-Century England', *The Journal of Economic History* 49 (1989), pp. 803–32.
13 Desan, *Making Money*, pp. 281–7, 293–4.
14 Quinn, 'Goldsmith-Banking', pp. 427.

Bibliography

Books, edited collections, and journal articles

Clapham, Sir John, *The Bank of England A History*, vol. 1 1696–1797 (Cambridge: Cambridge University Press,1945).

Desan, Christine, *Making Money: Coin, Currency, and the Coming of Capitalism* (Oxford: Oxford University Press, 2014).

Gauci, Perry, *The London Private Banker: A Social History, 1660–1825* (Oxford: Oxford University Press, 2025).

Joslin, D.M., 'London Private Bankers, 1720–1785', *The Economic History Review* 7 (1954), pp. 167–186.

Kadens, Emily, 'The Pitkin Affair: A Study of Fraud in Early English Bankruptcy', *American Bankruptcy Law Journal* 84 (2010), pp. 483–570.

Li, Ling-Fan, 'The Stop of the Exchequer and the Secondary Market for English Sovereign Debt, 1677–1705', *The Journal of Economic History* 79 (2019), pp. 176–200.

Melton, Frank T., 'Goldsmith Notes, 1654–1655', *Journal of the Society of Archivists* 6 (April 1978), pp. 30–31.

North Douglass, C., and Barry R. Weingast, 'Constitutions and Commitment: The Evolution of Institutions Governing Public Choice in Seventeenth-Century England', *The Journal of Economic History* 49 (1989), pp. 803–32.

Presnell, L.S., *Country Banking in the Industrial Revolution* (Oxford: Clarendon Press, 1956).

Quinn, Stephen, 'Banking before the Bank: London's Unregulated Goldsmith-bankers, 1660–1694' (unpublished thesis), University of Illinois (1994).

Quinn, Stephen, 'Goldsmith-Banking: Mutual Acceptance and Interbank Clearing in Restoration London', *Explorations in Economic History* 34 (1997), pp. 411–32.

Richards, R.D., *The Early History of Banking in England* (London: Routledge, 2012 reprint).

Roseveare, Henry, 'Prejudice and Policy: Sir George Downing as Parliamentary Entrepreneur', in D.C. Coleman and Peter Mathias (eds.), *Enterprise and History: Essays in Honour of Charles Wilson* (Cambridge: Cambridge University Press, 1984), pp. 135–50.

Roseveare, Henry, *The Financial Revolution 1660–1760* (London: Longman, 1991).

Turner, Gareth David, 'English Banking in the Eighteenth Century: Bankers, Merchants and the Creation of the English Financial System' (unpublished thesis), Durham University (2015).

Index